walking with
the seasons

walking with the seasons

the wonder of being in step with nature

alice peck

CICO BOOKS
LONDON NEW YORK

For Duane and Tyl—my favourite walking companions, no matter the season ...

Published in 2024 by CICO Books
An imprint of Ryland Peters & Small Ltd
20–21 Jockey's Fields   341 E 116th St
London WC1R 4BW   New York, NY 10029

www.rylandpeters.com

10 9 8 7 6 5 4 3 2 1

Text © Alice Peck 2024
Design © CICO Books 2024
For picture credits, see page 128

A CIP catalog record for this book is available
from the Library of Congress and the British Library.

ISBN: 978-1-80065-295-8

Printed in China

Commissioning editor: Kristine Pidkameny
Editor: Kristy Richardson
Designer: Geoff Borin
Art director: Sally Powell
Creative director: Leslie Harrington
Head of production: Patricia Harrington
Publishing manager: Penny Craig

MIX
Paper from
responsible sources
FSC® C106563

Contents

Introduction 6

Introduction

Weather, seasons, and dog companions have changed, yet I have taken pretty much the same walk every morning for over a decade, often with my husband, sometimes alone, or with my son or a friend. Depending on the day, on my path around New York Harbor I might see cormorants diving, Japanese maples budding, freshly hatched finches, huge hibiscus flowers filled with bees, ice-covered branches, or at least one soccer ball floating near the shore (there is always a soccer ball).

I love the ritual of my daily walk. Not only the familiarity of the landscape and my known route within it, but also the fleeting changes that come with each month, day, or hour—the shrouds of hazy mist, an escaped budgie, the melody of the ringing buoys, the treasures presented by each moment. These walks are the foundation of this book—a sensory and experiential map for being with each season, from spring to summer to autumn to winter. This guide will accompany you not only through nature, but through understanding, embodiment, and contemplation.

Why Do We Walk?

All this walking helps me to sort out my life—my daily mix of worries, hopes, concerns, and dreams, both large and small. In today's increasingly urbanized and technological world, we are surrounded by a tangled disharmonious mass of information. Walking is a linear action we can take in a world that is no longer linear.

In *Walking: One Step at a Time*, Erling Kagge wrote, "In Sanskrit, walking is not only a metaphor for time but also for 'knowing' or *gati*." In this sense, every word that means "walk" also means to "know." I have come to know my route with all my senses—the things never-before experienced, like yellow ducklings and linden trees blooming with a burst of sweet scent, the things no longer there, like ancient apple trees and snowmen, and all the surprises along the way, from shooting stars to woodcocks dancing or a white sparrow on the wing.

There are so many words for walking—amble, hike, march, journey, parade, saunter, shuffle, step, stride, strut, trek, trudge, wander, ambulate, lumber, meander, pace, promenade, roam, rove, stroll, scuff, shamble, slog, stalk, stump, toddle, traipse, tramp, traverse, tread, troop, and wend one's way ... but what does it mean to walk with the seasons?

Walking with Attention and Intention

As much as we may walk to arrive somewhere, we need to be where we are when we are walking, or we will miss the magic. Instead of walking through the seasons as they progress from spring to summer to autumn to winter and back to spring, I have made a conscious effort to write about walking *with* the seasons. Essentially, this an attempt to slow my pace and hopefully the reader's as well. It is a reminder to be present and mindful—not just think about being present and mindful, which is what I so often do. Instead, we can challenge ourselves to walk with intention as we pay attention.

When we walk with the seasons, we return to our inextricable connection and interconnection with nature. The natural world is many things—mercurial, beautiful, cruel, amorphous—but it is never boring. For me that constant state of transition sparks awe. It is a thrill, and a challenge, to stay with each moment, as ephemeral as it may be, until it is gone.

Your Walking Companion

As I wrote, I was inspired by Japanese *saijikis*—poetical seasonal almanacs observing nature, heaven, earth, and animals used in haiku and other forms of poetry. I also spent a lot of time perusing copies of the *Old Farmer's Almanac*: "Seasons are determined by the direction of Earth's tilt in relation to the Sun and the angle of the Sun's light as it strikes Earth!" But of course, there is much more to it.

Our minds, bodies, and spirits are shaped by the time we spend outdoors connected to place and time, nature and season. And this shaping takes many forms, from the physical to the spiritual to simple moments of delight. That is why I have tried to incorporate a surprise in each chapter, a new point of view, a scientific wonder, or maybe just a little fun. I have interwoven these with new ways to walk—beneficial activities, meditations, advice, and inspiration—from walking mantras to surprising brain and body benefits, and passages for reflection. I am hoping readers will apply these to their walks, new and familiar, quick and rambling, real and imagined.

So, no matter where, how, and when you walk, I am grateful to you for joining me as I wander through the notion of walking with (not through, against, or despite) the seasons. Together we can explore the poetry, science, mystery, and practicalities of what happens to our minds, bodies, and spirits when we put one foot in front of the other.

CHAPTER 1

A Spring Walk ...

Spring approaches with harbingers of warmer days to come—robins, mockingbirds, and thrushes resume their morning song as they nest and early, gold buds give way to new, green leaves, and blossoms. The earliest wildflowers—ephemeral trillium, bluebells, snowdrops, and trout lilies provide sustenance for the first pollinators of the season—bees, butterflies, and even beetles. Closer to the earth, new morels and puffballs emerge on damp days and nightcrawlers on very wet ones, as fiddleheads unfurl with warming breezes and cerulean skies.

Although all the seasons are the same length in terms of calendar days, spring seems somehow shorter, more swiftly fading, and transitory. The world sparks into life as the memories of winter linger.

How Happiness Leads to Joy

How often have you been frustrated—perhaps with yourself, co-workers, or a family member—and announced, "I need to take a walk"? And when you do, when you get outdoors among the blooming chestnuts trees or the emerging spring flowers in your neighborhood, you seem to walk away from negative thoughts and arrive at a better state of mind. Even with the first few steps you can feel yourself physically move out from a negative state into a positive one, from unhappy to happy. It turns out there is a science to this.

TRY THIS ...

A green space doesn't have to be a forest or a hiking trail. Seek out the unexpected—even in cities you can find "secret" green spaces like churchyards, botanic gardens, or areas near train stations.

We are significantly and quantifiably happier after walking in nature. There is a marked difference in the quality of experience between ten minutes of walking through a park, among sunlight and birdsong, cherry blossoms and May breezes, and an equal amount of time spent on a treadmill in a windowless gym. Myriad scientific studies by psychologists, neuroscientists, and physicians around the world offer evidence demonstrating how walking in nature affects our happiness, and some of it is quite startling.

A few years ago, a research team from Stanford University discovered walking for about an hour and a half in "non-urbanized settings" lessened depression, stress, and anxiety, as well as quieting persistent negative thoughts. Not only did these walks diminish ruminative thinking, but they also lowered the risk for mental illness both in the short and long term. Interestingly, the same amount of time spent in an urban environment (think concrete and traffic) had no impact on negative thoughts and very little on depression. Consider this the next time you feel stuck in a pattern of self-doubt or sorrow—seek out somewhere flourishing and green to walk.

Exercise

Does this happiness theory apply to you? Try this experiment: for at least fifteen minutes a day for a week, walk outdoors in the greenest place you have access to, with no purpose other than walking. Notice your mood before and after.

Then, as you walk, put a little bounce in your step! Another study showed how people who simply *imitate* a happy style of walking—swinging their arms, taking deep breaths, smiling, even skipping—can speedily and profoundly change their moods, feel happier, and improve their sense of life purpose. You might call it, "Acting as if ..."

There is something even more surprising about walking than simple happiness—joy! In her book, *Words for the Heart*, Maria Heim describes joy as "... different from happiness in that it seems to come from outside and hit us unawares ... unlike happiness it is a short-term episode and strikes unexpectedly." I would add that we can seek and find happiness if we apply ourselves, but joy—that moment of interconnected and unexpected bliss and presence—is a gift.

Aim for joy in your walks—take unfamiliar routes, allow yourself to be surprised by the new and the new ways of seeing the familiar. Sometimes those astonishing moments of joy can come from things we have seen many times—a favorite forsythia bursting into bloom, a pair of swans we have watched all spring swimming past with their fresh-hatched cygnets, or the way samaras whirl down from a beloved maple tree.

"Joy shakes me like the wind that lifts a sail ..."

Clarissa Scott Delany, "Joy"

A Joyful Walking Meditation

As you walk, imagine yourself as a sail. Allow yourself to be filled with the winds of joy, carrying you in unexpected directions and back to your delightful self. As you receive this joy, offer it outward in what Buddhists call *mudita* or "taking joy in the joy of others."

Consider the words of meditation teacher Sharon Salzberg: "One way to cultivate greater sympathetic joy is to connect with happiness in our own life ... Like any kind of generosity of spirit, joy for others depends on the feeling of inner abundance that is distinct from how much one has materially or objectively in this world. The knowledge that our lives are worth something releases our capacity to care about others and rejoice in their success."

DID YOU KNOW ...

Another study from 2019 mapped even more benefits of walking outdoors—increased positive mindset, resilience because our levels of cortisol (our stress hormone) were significantly lowered, and more meaningful social interactions. So, walking in nature can not only make our minds happier, but improve our relationships with others as well.

Dogs Are Our Best Teachers

In her memoir *What Is a Dog?* Chloe Shaw has "felt many a problem solved in the quiet steady transmissions through a leash ... walking a dog is like walking your heart." Dogs are our best teachers when it comes to walking with the seasons. They pay attention to everything—from intriguing smells (some prettier than others) to elusive squirrels—and are usually far more interested in the journey than the destination.

Every dog I have ever loved has been happy to be wherever they are, whenever they were. Taking the dog out is an entire subset of walking and applies to all the seasons, but it seems spring is the most exciting time for dog walks. *Stinky things have thawed! New puppies in the neighborhood! Puddles! Poop!* (Everything is italicized and has an exclamation point when spoken in Dog—at least, that is how we translate it in our house.)

There is a difference between walking our dogs and solitary walks (or walks with human companions, which, of course, have their own benefits). When psychologist Amy Jackson-Grossblat and her colleagues at Andrews University studied the therapeutic benefits of dog owners interacting with their dogs, they uncovered some expected—and startling—results. Not only did spending time together appear to promote mindfulness and heightened awareness of the environment in humans, but people who walked mindfully with their dogs also experienced heightened self-awareness, which they were then able to transfer to other human relationships. This means more satisfaction within themselves, a greater connection with others and, also, a deeper sense of belonging and significant meaning within the cosmos.

"In walking dogs, my heart endures."

Chloe Shaw, *What Is a Dog?*

TRY THIS ...

Dogs are spectacular motivators. Even when we do not particularly feel like getting a bit of fresh air and exercise, we still need take the dog out. We'll never have the sensory abilities of our canine pals, but what we can do is learn from them—especially the acuity and specificity of their attention and engagement with the world as we walk together.

Jackson-Grossblat's conclusions teach us that a genuine therapeutic benefit can come from establishing "a sense of self as part-of-nature" and that the dogs we walk can be an extension of, or even a conduit to, that nature. The study goes even further by suggesting that walking the family dog offers "a direct and practical means of developing new life meanings, to address the problems of life, and confront existential issues."

A Sensory Experience

When it comes to paying attention and interacting with nature and other-than-human beings (or human ones, for that matter) dogs have a distinct advantage—they have millions more sensory receptors than humans. Their sense of touch is enhanced by their paws, muzzles, and noses, which are full of nerve endings. And, for most breeds, their ability to hear is far more developed. Dogs can hear far higher frequencies—often three times as much as an average adult human—which means they can pick up on sounds too subtle for human ears, like mice squeaking or moles moving below the ground, humming insects, a familiar car driving toward your home, or even approaching earthquakes.

Of course, when it comes to smell, dogs have the greatest advantage. They have far more olfactory receptor cells than humans, and a snout better designed for detecting scents and interpreting them. Not only can they pick up on the aroma of things we would expect— like cats, pollen, or a pocketful of treats—but human emotions too. It is up for debate whether dogs can smell danger, but they can certainly smell fear, and perhaps even joy, via chemicals like pheromones and hormones like adrenaline, which mammals (including humans) release when frightened, excited, or attracted.

Exercise

We can learn everything we need to know (and not know) about spiritual teaching through our interactions with dogs, especially when it comes to the Buddhist path away from suffering. This is known as the five ways of liberation: perfect faith, energy or persistence, mindfulness or memory, stillness or concentration, and wisdom. Dogs embody all these five characteristics—there is no better mindfulness teacher than a dog.

As you walk, try to engage the world around you with the spirit of a dog, as if for the first time or with what Zen teachers call "beginner's mind." Watch what dogs are drawn to—the scent of lavender, the hum of bees in a blossoming linden tree, a fresh patch of clover—and savor the moments when a happy dog sits and simply listens to the breeze. Remember that it is about more than attention, it is about connected compassion—those "transmissions through a leash." Walk *with* your dog, just as you walk with the seasons.

Paths to Healing

Akuna Robinson was the first Black man to achieve the "triple crown" for completing three of the most challenging US trails: the Pacific Crest, the Appalachian (shown right), and the Continental Divide. He embarked on this journey as veteran of the war in Iraq, suffering from post-traumatic stress disorder (PTSD) and mental health issues, and walked his way to back to health.

As in Robinson's case, studies show that PTSD symptoms were improved in over 70 percent of veterans who hiked in nature. But walking does not just heal trauma. When it comes to being a "super ager" (a person whose brain ages more slowly than their body), walking—especially in nature—has been shown to improve cognition and adaptability. It offers considerable hope for people at high risk for developing disease- or aging-related cognitive decline. To a lesser degree, studies show the same is true for younger adults whose thinking processes and mental flexibility were enhanced by simply taking a walk with nature.

According to Chorong Song of Kongju National University, walking in springtime in particular has been shown to have value, even in an urban park. It decreases activity of the sympathetic nervous system (our fight-or-flight response) and increases parasympathetic activity (our body's ability to relax), which means walking—especially in the spring— is an easy way to take steps toward being calm and in a better mood.

TRY THIS ...

You do not need to be an accomplished trail hiker to reap the benefits Robinson did. You can take small steps as you explore the natural world around you. Even a walk around a city block can change your entire day. And a day (or a week) spent hiking the Appalachian Trail, the Milford Track, or the Cliffs of Moher, might change your entire life!

"Getting out there in nature allowed me to be able to live again."

Akuna Robinson, *LA Times*

Light's Constant Change

Changes in season bring many signs of spring from emerging flora and fauna to warm breezes and cool nights. But the most significant of these is the change in light—the amount, as days lengthen, and the intensity, as the earth's angle toward the sun shifts. Where I live, the winter sunrises are breathtaking, but the sunsets, which are closer to the horizon in the spring, are majestic.

This astronomical definition of spring is marked by the spring equinox, which is near March 20 or 21 in the northern hemisphere and near September 22 or 23 in the southern. Meteorologists and climatologists base their definition on temperature cycles and climate trends but, when it comes to walking in the spring, I'm with the astronomers. I think we are influenced far more by light than by temperature (which can still be in tremendous flux, as anyone who has shaken snow from a forsythia bush or rushed to bring potted seedlings indoors before a spring ice storm can tell you). In fact, one could say that no matter the geography or climate, it is the earth's angle in relationship to the sun that marks the seasons' change.

Constant Change and Natural Rhythm

Everything moves toward the light as spring arrives—humans and other creatures, trees, and plants have circadian rhythms that respond to light cues.

More light in spring inhibits the production of melatonin—a hormone fostered by darkness and released in the brain at night, which controls the sleep–wake cycle of mammals. Melatonin has been recently discovered in certain plants as well. Because melatonin is ubiquitous across all kingdoms of life, it becomes a kind of common language or way of interkingdom communication—we are more inclined to rest, hibernate, or grow dormant in the darker months, especially winter.

Researchers have demonstrated time and again that for most people, the extended daylight that begins in spring and continues into summer boosts mood, wellbeing, and energy. The "happy hormone" dopamine (a neurotransmitter associated with attention, motivation, pleasure, and mood) tends to increase with more exposure to sunlight.

TRY THIS ...

When you wake up on a spring morning, do your best to get outside as soon as possible—even if it's just a quick walk around the block. If that is not an option, open the curtains and look outside. Soak up the light. This will lower your stress levels and increase both dopamine (see left) and serotonin (the other "happy" hormone).

Practice

If you have a regular meditation, prayer, or contemplation practice, try doing it outside. As you walk, pause at a bench or boulder, and sit quietly, being with the spring light or spring shadows (if it is a breezy day, it might be both!). Notice how light is all about change—the shifts, intensity, and interplay. Be with light just as light, and be with shadow just as shadow, as you consider American Transcendentalist Henry David Thoreau's question: "With all your science can you tell how it is—and whence it is, that light comes into the soul?"

Smell: A Sense of Interconnection

From walking past a freshly mowed field to the intoxicating scent of bluebells on a woodland stroll, so many fragrances of nature evoke feelings and memories.

Although indistinguishable by the human nose, no two flowers smell exactly the same. The chemistry of their volatile compounds and the elements they have interacted with, like other plants and weather, mix to give each flower a unique aroma.

Along with color and structure, flowers employ aroma (found in essential oils called ionones) to attract pollinators and discourage predators. Although the terminology sounds kind of clinical, the experience is anything but. Species of plants that are pollinated by bees and other flying insects, like lavender, clover, and cherry blossoms, tend to have sweeter scents, whereas those pollinated by beetles, like tulip trees, yarrow, and sunflowers, have a richer, muskier fragrance. It is important to note that, although bees get much of the credit, beetles comprise the largest group of pollinating creatures and are responsible for pollinating 88 percent of the 240,000 species of flowering plants.

"Nothing is more remarkable than smell ... just one whiff of a familiar scene, and the memories come rushing back, not piece by piece, but as a whole, with all the flavors of the original experience miraculously intact."

Lyall Watson, *Jacobson's Organ*

TRY THIS ...

If you are anxious or having trouble sleeping, try walking in a fragrant spot—near a neighbor's rose bushes or even pay a visit to a lavender farm (see opposite)—and allow the healing phytochemicals to shift your mood. And if you cannot leave the house, a bouquet of sweet-scented flowers near your bedside or on a nearby windowsill may help.

Interestingly, to lure pollinators, flowers with less colorful blooms like darker purples, shades of brown, and white, exude strong scents—some of which can be detected at distances of over a mile. Conversely, younger flowers not ready to release their pollen have a less powerful fragrance and, once a flower has been pollinated, the fragrance changes. These shifts in scent encourage pollinators to seek out their more pollen-rich kin, thus increasing the chances of reproductive success for the plant and ultimately the species.

Plants and trees not only use smell to help themselves, but to communicate with each other as well. For plants, scent is a way of communication—pine trees, for example, amplify their scent to deter predators (especially insects) and to warn neighboring trees of the impending danger.

Their fragrance is also helping us. There is a science behind why we love the scents of nature—terpenes! Scientists have found that phytochemicals produced (mainly) by trees have healing, anti-inflammatory effects and can help as chemotherapeutic agents in the treatment of various human diseases. There is even evidence that inhaling them can slow the growth of tumors. Other terpenes like linalool (found in orange blossoms and lavender) may reduce stress and help you sleep. And several more studies have shown what anyone who has taken a walk in a freshly mown meadow or walked beneath a lilac tree in bloom knows—that pleasant smells boost psychological wellbeing long after the blossoms have fallen.

In Praise of Cardigans and Sensible Shoes

One of the great things about walking, as opposed to most other exercise or endeavor, is you do not need a lot of *stuff*. The only thing that really matters are shoes because, no matter the season, nothing crushes the spirit of a walk more quickly than sore feet. You just need something comfortable, that keeps your feet dry, and protects them from the surfaces you are walking on.

Spring has all the weathers, so be prepared. I like to bring a bottle of water and a cardigan sweater (not as useful as a raincoat but somehow more companionable). Consider a rain poncho or an umbrella and, of course, take the sunshine into consideration as well—bring a hat or even some sun block.

Gear is important ... except when it's not. Sometimes it is nice to be cold because it reminds you where your edges are (see page 100). Likewise, sinking bare feet into spring grasses or sand can be a remarkable sensation (see page 57), fostering connection—and delight!

TRY THIS ...

One thing I have come to appreciate as I have gotten older is how useful a walking stick (or, even fancier, trekking poles) can be, especially if the paths I am walking on are slippery or uneven.

Forest Bathing

Being with trees can heal our minds, bodies, and spirits—especially in the spring, as the trees begin the work of photosynthesis; bare branches awaken into buds and emerge into leaves, cellular breath turning the longer hours of spring light into energy.

In the early 1980s, Tomohide Akiyama, the director of the Japanese Ministry of Forestry and Fisheries, first coined the term *shinrin-yoku*. It means "making contact with and taking in the atmosphere of the forest" or "forest bathing." Another English definition of "bathe" is "to suffuse or permeate" and I love that concept—instead of walking into a forest, allow the forest to walk into us, to permeate our senses and spirits.

People have been forest bathing since they took their first walk in the woods, so the concept goes by many names. Consider the term *friluftsliv*, invented by the famous Norwegian playwright Henrik Ibsen in the 1850s. He used the term to describe the value of spending time in remote locations for spiritual and physical wellbeing. A century and a half later, scholar Dag T. Elgvin described friluftsliv as "the total appreciation of the experience one has when communing with the natural environment ... At its heart is the full identification and fulfillment of body and soul one experiences when immersed in nature."

Trees are literally greater than ourselves ...
Trees connect us directly to the life
of more-than-human nature.

Rupert Sheldrake, *Science and Spiritual Practices*

A physiological and psychological practice, by whatever name, forest bathing is a way of connecting with nature by breathing and walking among trees. It has been shown to elicit positive benefits like reducing anxiety and depression and boosting immunity and mood, self-esteem, life satisfaction, and happiness. Most interestingly, it is credited with raising awareness of, and strengthening compassion, for ourselves and for others. I think that is really important to remember—forest bathing is about more than us, it is about us in concert with more-than-human nature. As we support it, it supports us. It is about reciprocity.

Like walking, forest bathing is relatively accessible—it is as simple as accepting the presence of a tree, or lots of trees, into your full consciousness—the place between where your skin ends, and the world begins. Forest bathing is about being actively engaged by the place we are in, as we are in it. It is about the trees of course—the spring magnolia, dogwood, and newly green pine and cedar—but there is so much more to forest bathing. Through interconnection with the trees, you can be present with all of nature, from plants and fungi that need the rich soil of the woods to all the creatures that depend on the ecosystem of the forest.

Magic Numbers in Minutes and Miles

Most of us do not have the luxury of Henry David Thoreau's "four hours a day at least—and it is commonly more than that—sauntering through the woods and over the hills and fields, absolutely free from all worldly engagements." The average American walks 4,500 steps a day, or roughly 2 miles (3km). People in the UK and Ireland have them beat with an average step count of about 5,500 steps. And Hong Kong takes the lead with almost 7,000 average steps per day. Children and teenagers tend to accrue more, and the number of steps usually decreases as we age.

Because it is so easily gathered by smart watches and other tracking devices, there is a lot of fascinating data linked to our wellbeing and the number of steps we take. Japan's Ministry of Health, Labor and Welfare recommends an average of 9,000 steps, yet the UK's National Obesity Forum considers 8,000 steps per day the optimum number. Other research from the US tells us that women in their seventies who manage as few as 4,400 steps a day reduced their risk of premature death by up to 40 percent and steady declines in dementia incidence risk were associated with 9,800 steps per day, but even 3,800 at higher intensity made a difference. I could go on ...

TRY THIS ...

What if you do not want to be tethered to your watch or tracker? What if you want to leave your devices at home and just go for a walk while making sure you are reaping the many benefits? You can count your steps. Or consider another unit of measure—perhaps until the streetlights come on or until your feet are about to hurt. I recommend selecting a destination or distance and being with the steps instead of counting them.

Everyone, from athletes and neuroscientists to physiotherapists, and psychologists, has an opinion about how many miles or minutes we should walk. So, what is the magic number of steps?

Most of us, especially those with smart watches or fitness tracking devices, would immediately reply "Ten thousand." However, that number is not a scientific one at all—it originated with the 1964 Tokyo Olympic Games and the marketing of a mass-produced pedometer called the Manpo-kei, which means "10,000 steps meter." Over the years, people adopted this arbitrary number, but the science directs us elsewhere.

Quality not quantity

Instead of steps, consider time and effort ...

- The World Health Organization and the US Department of Health and Human Services recommend 150 minutes per week of moderate-intensity aerobic exercise, such as brisk walking, which can be divided into however many steps you like.
- Studies published in the Journal of American Medicine and Neurology recommend 30 minutes a day to lower the risk of dementia, cancer, heart disease, and even death.
- If you get up and move for a remarkably specific 21.43 minutes each day of the week, you cut your risk of dying from all causes by one-third, according to the US Centers for Disease Control and Prevention.

Ultimately the best number is up to you—but wherever you land, pick up the pace! It has been shown that people who walked more quickly, with more intensity even for shorter periods of time, reaped the best physical and psychological benefits.

Practice

We can apply some of the basics of meditation practice to quantity and quality of walking. One way to do this is to pay attention not to your device but to your breath as walk. Consciously notice when you inhale and exhale. Pay attention to the sensation of oxygen coming in through your nose. Do you notice a rhythm? How many steps sync up with your inhale? Your exhale?

Now try a more formal practice: pursed-lip breathing. Slowly inhale through your nose and gently exhale through pursed lips. This breathing technique can regulate your breathing because you inhale and exhale more air. Pursed lip breathing makes it easier to perform physical activities and reduces stress.

CHAPTER 2

A Summer Walk ...

Summer walks are an adventure unto themselves, the warmth
and sunshine providing ample reason to linger and observe.
The promises of spring are fulfilled as the gardens and parks
burst into bloom with butterfly bushes and hibiscus the size
of dinner plates, while beach grasses rustle with abundance.
Fledglings become expert fliers and goslings grow almost
indistinguishable from geese. Algae paints the rocks near shore
bright green as laughing herring gulls scour for nits and bits.
Rain and even thunderstorms offer relief instead of intrusion,
and every breeze is welcomed.

Summer walks are slower with the longer days and heavier
air, tempering our pace and grounding us in time and place.

The Wandering Mind

Walking for the pure sake of walking with no real destination—wandering, ambling, or sauntering—could be considered a subset of walking—an activity or practice onto itself.

According to a recent study from Stanford University, walking increases divergent and imaginative thought while decreasing rational and linear thinking. "Walking opens up the free flow of ideas, and it is a simple and robust solution to the goals of increasing creativity and increasing physical activity." Especially walking outdoors. The study produced the insight that walking allows the mind to wander more spontaneously, having "increased the activity of associated memory".

So, if you are pondering a particular question, you are not just thinking about the solution but allowing in all the thoughts around that issue. This is beneficial to all types of problem solving, whether it is a personal dilemma or a math problem, in part because non-directed walking seems to ease the competition between thoughts and memories, allowing new ideas to emerge. It is kind of like letting go of stiffness and resistance, much like the difference between trying to ride a bicycle and just doing it.

Sometimes it does not matter where we go, just going somewhere—literally walking away from the problem or the distractions of our devices and responsibilities—allows us to wander into the wide-open spaces of our minds.

Walking Toward Knowledge

What is even more fascinating is this phenomenon also happens in relationships when we walk without a predetermined route or destination with a companion, together, side-by-side, as researchers studying

"... there are some essential mysteries in the world and thereby a limit to calculation, to plan, to control. To calculate on the unforeseen is perhaps exactly the paradoxical operation that life most requires of us."

Rebecca Solnit, *A Field Guide to Getting Lost*

robotics in Kyoto, Japan found. According to Reggio Emilia (an educational philosophy and pedagogy focused on early education), "All wisdom is gained by asking, listening, and walking." Alice Wexler, author of *Arts Education Beyond the Classroom*, went on to say that in this learning paradigm, "Walking without a destination is the process of learning by listening." Greek philosophy provides an elegant example—Plato, Aristotle, and Socrates all walked together as they pondered, studied, and theorized. That is why, according to Wexler, "Walking toward knowledge" has become one of Reggio Emilia's several metaphors. The phrase suggests that giving up certainty and walking without a destination "allows the search to take precedence over the known."

Practice

According to Jon Kabat-Zinn, the psychologist who introduced mindfulness-based stress reduction (MBSR) to the Western world, "Everything that unfolds, unfolds now, and so might be said to unfold in the nowscape." He incorporates the nowscape into a practice he teaches called choiceless awareness, or "the state of unpremeditated, complete presence without preference, judgment, effort, or compulsion."

We can apply this understanding of the nowscape to walking with the seasons. As you wander do not just be with the place you are walking—be the walk itself. Let go of ruminations or to-do lists, worries, or plans. As you do, notice what flows into your thoughts, your consciousness ... and what drifts away. Abide fully in the nowscape.

TRY THIS ...

Settle on a question that has been stuck in your mind—it could be about a career or relationship choice or something more specific, like how to move forward in a writing or art project, or a negotiation. Now, go for a walk—ideally without destination or a specific time for return. Do not dwell on the problem, but do not push it out of your mind or conversation either. Let it float in and out of your consciousness as if a cloud in the sky. Did wandering and allowing the search to take precedence reveal the answer? Did it settle the disagreement?

Nightwalking with Fireflies, Moonflowers, and Bats

My favorite walks are on summer evenings, when the air is so full of fireflies I can't tell where they end, and the stars begin. Like Aimee Nezhukumatathil, author of *World of Wonders*, "I know I will search for fireflies all the rest of my days ... They blink on and off, a lime glow to the summer night air, as if to say: I am still here, you are still here ..."

Night walking encourages a different pace. The world is calmer—traffic and airplanes and human chatter quieten, vision becomes less dominant, different kinds of sounds and smells intensify and come into focus. Writing about walking at night, Nina Morris of the University of Edinburgh pointed out that, "Darkness also forces one to question how one's body is in relation to that which surrounds, challenging one's human sense of bodily presence and boundary."

Every type of walk changes if you try it at night. If you wander by the ocean, a little moonlight can make a big difference to navigation, and the sounds traveling across the water are intensified. If you walk in the city, you'll encounter fewer humans and less noise and air pollution. If you are intrepid and walk in the woods at night, you are likely to encounter both wildlife and a remarkable aura of quiet and calm.

Encounters at Dusk

We tend to forget that nature does not end at night—instead there is a whole other world to encounter on night walks—glow worms and skunks, possums, and phosphorescent algae. One stellar nighttime performer is the barred owl, whose idiosyncratic hoot sounds as if they are asking, *"Who cooks for you? Who cooks for you now?"* Canadian geese (see above) honk and fly on late summer skies as they migrate south, favoring the calmer winds and cooler thermals of the night air to reduce exertion and avoid daytime predators. Ghostly moths appear, those forgotten pollinators, not as vivid as bees or as gaudy as butterflies. Their colors are muted to blend in with their surroundings during the day, while they sleep on bark or leaves, remaining still to avoid predators.

There is an entire botany of night-blooming flowers and other nocturnal plants that we would miss if we limited our walks to daylight: moonflower, datura, gladioli, phlox,

TRY THIS ...

Darkness is an endangered state. There is just not enough of it anymore, especially in cities, so if it is safe to do so, turn off the lights! Not only will it help you focus your attention of the nighttime experience, but you can reduce the effect of human-made light on migratory birds and pollinating insects, which can be terribly disruptive.

Practice

In *Learning to Walk in the Dark*, Barbara Brown Taylor encourages us to drop our expectations and preconceived notions about the dark. Being comfortable in the dark—and the darker areas of life—is an ever-changing process that is different for everyone. She writes that "endarkenment, like enlightenment, is a work in progress ... learning to walk in the dark has allowed me to take back my faith, removing it from the glare of the full solar tradition to recover by the light of the moon."

As you walk at night, carry this idea of "endarkenment" with you. How can the moonlight on your path light up the shadowy, frightening, or painful challenges in your life?

jasmine, and orchids that only bloom after sunset. And then there is the evening primrose (see right) ...

If you time it well, and you are fortunate enough to find one along your path, you can watch this bashful bloom open in real time. With a quiver the sepals (the green exterior of the flower) move downward and the bud gradually begins to open. Finally, the pale-yellow flower stretches out until it is about 4–6in (10–15cm) in circumference. As it opens, it exudes a lovely fragrance that invites its preferred pollinator, the pretty pink primrose moth.

The moths, in turn, have their own nighttime predator: bats. They come out to hunt as the sun goes down, hopefully going after other night-flying insects like mosquitos instead.

Attuning to the Sounds of Nature

Physics describes sound as a vibration, which transmits as an acoustic wave through a medium like a gas, liquid, or solid. In terms of human physiology and psychology, sound is how the ear receives those acoustic waves and the brain perceives them. The dictionary defines the word sound as "noise, what is heard, sensation produced through the ear", and is derived from Old French, the word *son* meaning "sound, musical note, voice". I love the idea that every noise or sound has a song at its heart.

As you walk, listen. Attune yourself to all of nature. The sounds of footsteps as you walk; the splat-suck in mud, the crunch of fallen leaves, the muffled thud in snow. Hear the variety of wind; the gusts over fields and breezes through the trees. (The sound of leaves rustled by the wind has a name: susurration, one of my favorite words.) Notice seasonal change, how the songs of spring morph into songs of summer via thunder crash, toad croak, and bobolink trill. And how autumn grows quieter, as most birds finish mating for the year and cicadas quiet their scritch. Notice the creak of trees and the patter of hail in winter, and all the other sounds we forget to pay attention to.

It is fascinating to ponder the sounds that humans cannot naturally hear. Elephants, whales, rhinoceros, giraffes, and alligators use infrasonic calls at a frequency too low for human ears. Likewise, bats, praying mantis, dolphins, dogs, frogs and toads, and even bacteria, emit sounds which we can only hear if amplified. Mice emit ultrasonic vocalizations at too high a frequency for us to hear, but when recorded and played at lower frequencies and slower speeds, these pitch-shifted vocalizations are surprisingly reminiscent of birdsong, according to researchers from Washington University of Medicine.

"We are one huge universe
speaking and listening to itself."

Francis Lucille, *The Perfume of Silence*

The Importance of Birdsong

According to neuroscientist Emil Stobbe of the Max Planck Institute for Human Development, "The special thing about birdsong is that even if people live in very urban environments and do not have a lot of contact with nature, they link the songs of birds to vital and intact natural environments." Upon further analysis, Stobbe and his colleagues noticed a significant, positive association between observing and listening to birds and psychological wellbeing. This improved state of mind endured beyond the hearing birdsong, often for hours.

Similar studies have observed how even listening to a few minutes of recorded birdsong can ease anxiety, depression, stress, and even paranoia. Richard Sima, writing for the *Washington Post*, describes attention restoration theory—the hypothesis that the salubrious effect of being in nature "is good for improving concentration and decreasing the mental fatigue associated with living

in stressful urban environments. Natural stimuli, such as birdsong, may allow us to engage in 'soft fascination,' which holds our attention but also allows it to replenish." Hearing birdsong is also a glorious way to wake up!

Deep Listening

When it comes to conversation, deep listening is listening beyond the words—hearing not only with auditory intelligence but emotional intelligence and empathy. We can apply this to our walks in nature—hearing beyond the ordinary to the extraordinary.

The fourth-century, Taoist master Zhuangzi Chuang Tzŭ taught "In hearing do not use the ear, but the mind; do not use the mind but the chi (spirit). When you use the ear, the hearing stops there, and the mind cannot go further than the symbol; chi is something empty and waiting. Tao abides in the emptiness, and the emptiness is mind-fasting." The notion of mind-fasting—taking a break from the distractions and comforts that separate us from presence—is a fascinating one. When we starve ourselves of distractions, we arrive at a place of deepest listening, purely connected without interpretation or filtering.

"We cannot step outside life's songs. This music made us; it is our nature."

David George Haskell, *The Songs of Trees*

Pond Skippers and Puddle Jumpers

I live near New York Harbor and walk the same patch of coastline close to my home at least once a day, sometimes many times. It is never boring, offering up an ever-changing banquet for the senses. I have seen baby ducks, fog, cormorants and gulls, heard the song of buoy bells, watched an occasional hermit crab scuttle across the sand, and once found a seahorse washed up on shore. As with any place in nature, the more you look, the more you'll see.

Psychologists and neuroscientists alike agree that walking or living near bodies of water—blue spaces—has a positive and restorative influence on people. Spending time in, or even seeing blue spaces, diminishes stress and psychological pain. Articles have shown that mental and emotional wellbeing can be restored, and anxiety or mood disorders lessened.

Perhaps this is in part because all our senses engage differently when we are near bodies of water. Sounds carry much further across water, as birdsong and animal skitter are replaced by fish splash or wave crash. Even smells engage us differently, like the lovely low tide funk (the breakdown of marine algae), an evocative scent with a decidedly unpoetic name: dimethyl sulfide.

"The tides come in, and the tides go out—
but low or high, serene or tempestuous,
the sea is always full."

Jaimal Yogis, *Saltwater Buddha*

TRY THIS ...

Have you ever noticed that trees and buildings are rarely reflected in the ocean? While we can appreciate the psychedelic ripples of ocean wave patterns, their rhythmic crashing or foamy hiss, the brisk burn of salt spray on our cheeks, it takes a still, waveless surface like a lake or a pond to become a liquid mirror (see below). In this reflection, the water world echoes back an image of its own earthly surroundings. If you pass by a still body of water, try to focus on the reflections. Consider how it is just as much a reality as that which it reflects.

When blue spaces are combined with green, according to Andrea Mechelli of King's College London, the healing potential grows exponentially. "Canals and rivers contain not only water but also an abundance of trees and plants, which means their capacity to improve mental wellbeing is likely to be due to the multiple benefits associated with both green and blue spaces." The presence of birds, mammals, and aquatic life makes a difference as well, "as there is a positive association between encountering wildlife and mental wellbeing."

Even if you can't get to the sea, a lake, river, or canal on your walks, there is so much life in a simple puddle. Do not avoid them as you walk—celebrate them instead! They're nature's bird baths, a source of spackle for swallows building nests, and a hatchery for larvae and tadpoles. Butterflies seek out the moist mud that can be found around the puddle's edge, consuming nutrients like salts and amino acids and engaging in a behavior aptly called "puddling." "Puddle-wonderful" as E. E. Cummings wrote.

Practice

Whether you have access to the Pacific Ocean, a glacial pool, or simply a puddle on your park path, take a moment to pay attention to your body of water. Consider the words of the Hindu mystic Ramakrishna Paramahansa, who famously said, "The water and its bubble are one: the bubble has its birth in the water, floats on the water, and is ultimately resolved into water ... the one is finite and limited, the other is infinite; the one is dependent; the other is independent."

Consider how the bubble is a metaphor for our interconnected lives, our interconnected world— simultaneously relative and absolute.

"The landscapes in the sea change from season to season just as they do on land."

Michiko Ishimure, *Kugai Jodo*

The Delights of Rain and Earthing

There is really no such thing as bad weather—all weather is easier or more difficult to navigate—but walking in the rain is worth the effort. In the summer, it can be a benefit and not an inconvenience, especially in areas or times of drought. Sometimes a light rain can feel like a gift when we are walking on a hot summer's day. Plus, there is a silver (or colorful) lining to summer walks in the rain—the season with the most rainbows is summer.

Flowers and trees react to the changes in the weather, like high pressure and impending rain, by drooping and closing up their petals to protect their pollen—it can't be carried by wind or bees if it is washed away. I would say the same applies to humans. Our energy shifts in the rain and so does our experience of walking. There is a whole new world to see—the change of light and shadow under cloud cover, the colors of landscape through drizzle, and the ways trees turn their leaves to receive the rain.

"The mud is our pain, our suffering, our challenges. The lotus is our joy, our potential, our freedom. We can choose to see the mud as a barrier or as a fertilizer."

Pema Chödrön, *When Things Fall Apart*

TRY THIS ...

Remember to wear waterproof boots if you are walking long distances in rain or through mud. Some sort of textured sole is useful—the grip will prevent slipping. However, if you are experimenting with earthing, *do not* wear shoes with rubber soles, as they block the electromagnetic energy emitted by the Earth.

Petrichor

And then there is the fragrance of all of it combined—meadow and forest, kitchen garden or field—teeming soil when it gets soaked after a dry spell. Petrichor is the word for this smell of rain. It is a term derived from the Greek "petra" meaning stone and "ichor", which in Greek mythology refers to the golden fluid that flows in the veins of the gods. Petrichor infuses the air when the rain awakens bacteria in the soil. A chemical—a simple, organic molecule—called geosmin (literally meaning "earth odor") is released. It is a fragrance we tend to love, perhaps because it evokes a sense of fecundity and renewal, or fresh beginnings.

Grounding

Have you ever—rain or not—had the urge to take off your shoes and socks and stand on the ground? It might not be all in your head, but rather, perhaps in your feet. According to studies published by scientists from the University of California, Irvine, "Emerging scientific research has revealed a surprisingly positive and overlooked environmental factor on health: direct physical contact with the vast supply of electrons on the surface of the Earth." While modern life often prevents humans from direct contact with the Earth, research suggests that this "may be a major contributor to physiological dysfunction and unwellness. Reconnection with the Earth's electrons has been found to promote intriguing physiological changes and subjective reports of well-being."

Experiment with grounding yourself—walk barefoot outside, sit, or even sleep on the ground as a way of reconnecting to the Earth or "earthing". Nascent research is beginning to indicate that physically connecting with the Earth—whether walking and standing outside barefoot or using more elaborate conductive systems manufactured and sold to use indoors—may be a natural, basic, and yet powerfully effective way to combat chronic stress, inflammation, pain, insomnia, and lots of other common health disorders, even autoimmune and cardiovascular disease. It's been called "environmental medicine."

Practice

Take off your shoes and socks and stand on an unpaved patch of ground. If it feels weird to do this in dirt, try sand at the beach or a lawn in a park. If you are feeling daring, let your toes sink into the mud. Envision energy flowing into your body and out through your feet. Sense your relationship to the Earth, the planet. Breathe. Pause. Do you feel restored? Connected?

The Wonders of Creative Walking

When I am stuck in my work and can't see the forest for the pencils, I go for a walk. I'm not alone—in fact, I'm in very good company. It is said that when a visitor asked where poet William Wordsworth's study was, they were told "Here is his library, but his study is out of doors." Writers from Emerson to Dickens, musicians from Tchaikovsky and Beethoven to Mahler, philosophers from Aristotle to Rousseau, and poets like Wordsworth, Keats, and O'Hara have all relied on the power of walking to find direction and inspiration in their writing.

Neuroscientists and psychologists have shown that walking enhances creativity and problem-solving and even helps us produce new brain cells. Henry David Thoreau must have sensed this when he wrote: "Methinks that the moment my legs begin to move, my thoughts begin to flow." He agrees with neuroscientists Marily Oppezzo and Daniel L. Schwartz, who wrote, "Walking opens up the free flow of ideas, and it is a simple and robust solution to the goals of increasing creativity and increasing physical activity."

Just as walking inspires art, walking has become an artistic practice unto itself. "Walking artists" explore the connections between the body and mind, and even time and space, while others use walking to create a physical narrative or raise consciousness about issues. The Dadaists' and Surrealists' "deambulations" through Paris in the early 1920s were intended to achieve a state of hypnosis by walking, a disorienting loss of control. Even earlier, for Matsuo Bashō, the seventeenth-century Japanese haiku poet, walking and poetry were intrinsically linked. Whatever the origins, walking through and *with* a landscape can be a means toward self-expression.

"Sit. Walk. Write."

Natalie Goldberg, *The True Secret of Writing*

Footprints on the Landscape

For most of human history, we have been migratory, hunter-gatherers, walking toward food or walking away from weather and danger. Walking has always been about adaptation, and now—as we adapt to urbanization and climate change—walking is becoming a luxury or opportunity, rather than a necessity.

If we all walked more and drove less, we could have a vast impact on the Earth. According to the Environmental Protection Agency, if we all chose to walk (or bike) for half of our car trips of under a mile (1.5km), not only would we be healthier, but the planet would benefit too.

Americans would save millions in fuel costs and prevent about two million metric tons of carbon dioxide emissions from entering our atmosphere annually, decreasing air pollution (not to mention noise and traffic) exponentially. More importantly, this would have an impact on climate change as well: as CO2 levels increase, so do Earth's.

"Let no one say, and say it to your shame
That all was beauty here until you came."

Anonymous, *The Long Trail News*

In Step with Nature

Many languages do not have a word for nature, reflecting the intuitive belief that there is no distinction between us and our living environment—they are inextricably bound. Our feet are on the ground and the air is in our lungs. There is no other place to be than where we are.

Just as we interact with nature, nature interacts with us. The more we notice this, the more we can marvel at the myriad way we are entangled. Take, for example, how nature can serve as a clock to we humans. Eighteenth-century naturalist Carl Linnaeus discovered that different flowers open at different times during the day—a sort of flower clock. Based on times in his native Uppsala, Sweden:

Dandelions open at 5am
Waterlilies open at 7am
Ice plants open at 9am
Garden lettuce closes at 10am
Marigolds close at 3pm
Poppies and day lilies close at 7pm

In a less precise way I see this in my summer walks—zucchini blossoms open early and close at dusk, the marigolds perk up a little later in the morning, the dandelions tend to close after lunch and the poppies later in the day as dusk approaches.

Practice .

Erling Kagge wrote in *Walking: One Step at a Time*, "The longer I walk, the less I differentiate between my body, my mind, and my surroundings. The external and internal worlds overlap. I am no longer an observer looking at nature, but the entirety of my body is involved."

Put this into practice as you walk. Instead of separation—the terrain is too rough, it is too cold for a walk, the park is crowded—try feeling what connects you with the landscape. Allow yourself to be enveloped—the delight of a shade tree, the thrill of a breeze, a cacophony of crows.

How can you embody your presence in nature instead of disconnecting from it?

Pilgrimages and Circumambulation

From pilgrimages to the birthplace of the Buddha in Lumbini, Nepal (shown opposite), to the shrine of the Apostle Saint James in the Cathedral of Santiago de Compostela, Spain, leaving our day-to-day routines and traveling by foot to a holy site can be an act of reverence, restoration, and perhaps revelation.

TRY THIS ...

There is a value in walking the same path again and again. Think about this the next time you walk somewhere—not a special hike or a park stroll, but to the corner store or to pick up your mail. Imbue that walk with the same ceremony as a sacred walk. How does the "same old" become fresh and revelatory?

You do not have to travel to a new place. Many spiritual traditions practice circumambulation, which means walking in a circle around a meaningful shrine or object to express reverence or focus on prayer. Like the 32-mile (50km) hike around Mount Kailash in Tibet, or the 20-minute walk around the Kaaba at the center of the Grand Mosque in Mecca, there is meaning to be found in walking the same path many times.

My sacred place is not a shrine or ancestral mountain, but a pond. I have returned to Schoolhouse Pond in Cape Cod, Massachusetts, every summer for decades. As a child I played there with my siblings and my son learned to swim in those brackish waters. I have walked its shores more times than I can count, wondering, dreaming, and remembering. It is always the same, but always different—the experience becomes ever-richer with each visit.

CHAPTER 3

An Autumn Walk ...

After the slow motion of summer, autumn walks awaken the senses—or perhaps reawaken them. The satisfying crunch of leaves on pavement in all their red, orange, yellow, and ochre glory; the birds beginning to migrate—the finches and smaller birds at first, with the anticipation of farewell to mergansers and even herons to come; the weight and rot of fallen fruit—winey crabapples and stinky gingkoes—all delightful to foraging creatures, especially squirrels, mice, and industrious ants. Downpours and the hushed anticipation of snow on the way.

The moon has been in the sky all along, of course, but in autumn it seems to provide a confiding intimacy as the warm, fiery tones of the harvest moon give way to the frost moon and the first snowfall of winter.

The Pleasures of Companionship and Solitude

If asked to claim a favorite—walking alone or walking with companions—I would be hard-pressed to choose. They both have so much to recommend them. I love sharing and discussing observations when I walk near my home with my husband. And yet the chance to be alone with my thoughts when I go out walking by myself, or with our dog Pearl, always leads to an epiphany. I often say I do my best editing and writing while walking.

There are so many ways to walk together—in friendly one-on-one companionship or as a group learning about a landscape or touring city sites, marching for a cause you believe in, celebrating in a parade, or walking with a purpose like hiking or picking up litter.

It turns out walking with community has some surprising and also logical benefits. According to longevity research from the University of California San Diego, adults living in less car-dependent and more "walkable" neighborhoods tend to not only be healthier, but have a deeper sense of community as the result of neighborly interaction. They also tended to be healthier, and their wellbeing improved. Recently, the US Surgeon General advised that isolation and loneliness contribute to a 29 percent increased risk of heart disease, 32 percent increased risk of stroke, a 50 percent increased risk of developing dementia among older adults, and an increased risk of premature death by more than 60 percent. That is quite significant! So, seek out a housemate, a friend from the local library, or acquaintance from across the street and take a walk together!

"In the course of a walk, we usually find out something about our companion, and this is true even when we travel alone."

Thomas A. Clark, *In Praise of Walking*

TRY THIS ...

For those who like to walk in good company, the rising popularity of walking festivals is a happy phenomenon. They differ from group walks in that there is an element of hosting—sharing one's landscape (and local foods) with visitors and strangers—as well as a celebratory aspect. The UK hosts events in locations from the Yorkshire moors to the Devon coast throughout September, and Dartmoor incorporates a wheelchair off-roading experience into their festival as well. A few minutes on the internet will show you that these festivals are not limited to the UK. You can find events from Martinique to South Korea, from Canada to Spain, and pretty much everywhere in between all year long.

Alone and Together

Other studies have shown that group walks (especially in nature) relieve stress and reduce depression, and help us thrive. As an introvert who savors aloneness when I walk, I'd argue that you can reap these benefits on your own as well. But if you are walking by yourself, really walk by yourself. In his book *Digital Minimalism*, Cal Newport points out that "At the slightest hint of boredom, you can now surreptitiously glance at any number of apps or mobile-adapted websites that have been optimized to provide you an immediate and satisfying dose of input from other minds. It's now possible to completely banish solitude from your life." That is the opposite of solitude. So be a good walking companion, even to yourself, and do your best to stay present.

Always Hand in Hand

Vietnamese Zen master Thich Nhat Hanh incorporated walking into much of his teaching and often recited versions of his poem from *Call Me by My True Names* instructing:

Take my hand.
We will walk.
We will only walk.
We will enjoy our walk.
We will enjoy our walk
without thinking of arriving anywhere ...
We walk for ourselves.
We walk for everyone
always hand in hand.

As you walk, alone or together, recite these words in your mind. If you are walking alone, think of the greater "we" of the interconnected world and universe, and if you are walking in companionship apply the "we" to those with whom you travel the same path. Either way, just walk without thoughts of departure or arrival.

"The pleasure of a walk in the woods and fields is enhanced a hundred-fold by some little knowledge of the flowers which we meet at every turn."

Mrs. William Starr Dana, *How to Know the Wild Flowers*

The Names of Things

Orange and gold in the autumn, crackled brown in the winter, light green in the spring—a maple leaf is still a leaf, whatever the color. There is something in the consistency of names for things, despite their impermanence and constant transformation, that is steadying and delighting.

For me, language—especially finding intriguing new words—helps me see things through a different lens. In fact, I love to collect words; I enjoy learning the names of things. Perhaps it creates a sense of connection or an illusion of mastery, but there is a thrill in the naming, whether it be birds, streets, or even parts of trees—canopy, heartwood, samara ...

Although I have a habit of making up names when I do not know the real ones—rock gulls and fire flowers come to mind—there is satisfaction in the biological nomenclature (scientific naming), especially when it comes to botanical terms.

Known as the "father of modern taxonomy," eighteenth-century Swedish botanist, zoologist, and physician Carl Linnaeus formalized the modern system of binomial nomenclature (naming organisms). There is a wealth of information in these taxonomic names. Some tell of healing potential, like *Asclepias syriaca* (milkweed), which refers to Asclepias, the Greek god of medicine, because historically its many medicinal uses included wart removal and treating lung disease. Some taxonomic names seem to be ones of convenience, like *Cucurbita moschata* (squash or pumpkin), meaning "musky gourd". Others are just intriguing and odd, like *Procyon lotor* (racoon or before-the-dog washer) and *Tarache delecta* (the delightful bird-dropping moth).

Roots and Repetition

Any repeated word or words can become a mantra. They can be chanted, whispered, or simply held in mind, but to be a mantra, it must be imbued with meaning. It is a spiritual discipline that reaches into all religions. Christians recite the rosary, Muslims repeat the word "bismillah," and the Hindu "Om," one of the best-known mantras, is considered the primordial sound of the universe.

Researchers from SSGM and MIT universities studied the brain during meditation sessions when the word Om was recited. People who were new to meditation were asked to close their eyes and chant loudly for thirty minutes. EEGs recorded brain activity before and after the mantras were recited. The analysis revealed that after mantra practice, theta rhythm (the brain waves underlying learning, memory, and spatial navigation) was significantly increased. Other studies have indicated a reduction in cortical arousal (vigilance, wakefulness, and increased heart rate) during a state of relaxation like meditation. Perhaps Om indeed has specific vibrational qualities.

Practice

There is no rule that says you can't create your own mantra. As you walk, choose what the Japanese call your "true word" evoking season, place, or maybe a state of mind you want to attain. Repeat the word as you focus your concentration and perhaps connect it to each step as you walk. Perhaps it is "Osprey, osprey, osprey ..." or "Samara, samara, samara ..." or "Patience, patience, patience ..."

The Importance of Names

Since the meanings of words impact our thoughts, it is important as we learn the names of plants and birds, fungi, and fossils, to consider their roots. There are hidden (and sometimes not so hidden) connotations that lurk in many of these names. Fortunately, botanists, ornithologists, and etymologists are doing something about it, by renaming or returning to the scientific name, like the *Lymantria dispar* ("gypsy" moth), for example. Likewise, they've revisited common bird names, pointing out many that honor problematic historical figures, and have taken action. The American Ornithological Society recently rechristened a small species of songbird—McCown's longspur, which was named after a Confederate American Civil War general who was complicit in genocide—the thick-billed longspur. Because of the work of organizations like Bird Names for Birds that are working to change this, many more will follow.

Healing the Wound
No One Can See

For some of us, autumn marks beginnings—the new school year, the harvest—but for others, the summer's end signifies a loss. When we are grieving, sometimes it can feel as though we are frozen; our familiar paths are gone, and we don't know how to move forward. Nobody can tell another how to grieve—there is certainly no one right way to do so—but I also know walking has helped me move my body through the saddest of times and helped my mind and heart begin to thaw.

That is akin to the experience my Brooklyn neighbor Danelle Davis had after she unexpectedly lost her lover and best friend of eighteen years. They both loved the outdoors and often hiked together. A friend told her about Destination Backcountry Adventures, which offered a Healing Hike with birth, grief, and end-of-life doula, Bilen Berhanu, to the Catskill Mountains (shown opposite). It sounded like exactly the thing that might help Danelle through the difficult phase she felt stuck in. "The hike was difficult, in a number of ways, but with the help of the most supportive people and guides I'd ever encountered, I made it to the top of my first 3,500ft (1,066m) peak. I thought of my missing partner the whole way, how proud he would have been of me. How he would have enjoyed the beauty of the forest."

Danelle went on to describe how, "The biggest tragedy of my life had led me to one of the most beautiful days I'd ever experienced. It felt healing, it felt like something positive. It gave me the strength to go on."

"The forest and mountains welcome you, they hear you—and if you let them in, they can help to heal you too."

Danelle Davis

Stones, Feathers, Trash, and Sticks

Paying attention and focusing on finding a specific type of object as you walk provides a delightful type of engagement and joy. Most of us know the thrill of gathering golden leaves or fallen acorns in autumn or picking up pretty shells or stones from the beach.

What to Pick Up

I especially love finding beach glass—not only is it pretty, but it is also such a remarkable illustration of the human/nature cycle. Someone litters and it comes back to us as treasure. Glass is made from sand, it becomes an object that we use, it ends up in the sea—nature's lapidary, grinding and smoothing off the hard edges of civilization—before giving it back to us, polished and beautiful. Something as unsightly and sad as broken glass becomes a gem for gathering.

It turns out the truism of little children with their pockets full of stuff is rooted in science. The desire to collect things is hardwired; for most of human history we were gatherers, until things fundamentally changed with the invention of agriculture approximately 10,000 years ago, yet our foraging impulse has endured.

Another interesting phenomenon goes with this—the ancient impulse to share, whether this be information, tools, or food. My toddler friend Aubrey is a perfect example. Whenever he takes a walk with us, he carefully chooses the most enticing leaves—selected to a standard and specificity only he can quite determine—and presents them to us with great glee. Sometimes, he will offer many, one-by-one-by-one until our pockets are full, and something else captures his fascination—"Train!"

"and Maggie discovered a shell
that sang so sweetly she couldn't
remember her troubles"

E.E. Cummings, "maggie and milly and molly and may", *95 Poems*

TRY THIS …

Some things to gather as you walk in autumn:

- Wishing stones: gray or black rocks with an unbroken line (usually quartz or calcite) that goes all the way around.
- Heart rocks: just like their name, they are shaped like hearts and are a sign of love.
- Pennies: remember the nursery rhyme, "Find a penny, pick it up, all the day long you'll have good luck."
- Feathers: perhaps they're a message from loved ones or angels, or maybe a miracle in their own right. In many cultures, people interpret fallen feathers as messages from loved ones who have passed on.
- And, of course, beach glass!

What to Leave Behind

There are things that should never disturbed or picked up. The adage "Take nothing but pictures, leave nothing but footprints" is one we best heed. Leaving nothing behind can apply to trash of course, but other sorts of human disruption as well, like radio noise or idling car exhaust, especially when visiting less-populated areas.

So much is better admired and untouched, from spider webs to cultural artifacts. We know not to damage living trees but should remember to leave fallen ones alone too—they are likely home to a complex community of lifeforms like fungi and foxes, salamanders and shrews. Once the leaves have fallen and wasps' nests become visible, I am often tempted to retrieve one because they are so intricately constructed and magical. I refrain, because in autumn even the nests that seem empty may still contain some inhabitants. This "let it be" rule applies to large rocks as well, and birds' nests too, because some species—particularly larger birds of prey like eagles and hawks, but also geese and hummingbirds—return to their nests year after year.

Uitwaaien: Loving the Wind

The wind is one of my favorite things. Breezes through an open window, a hint of winter in autumn air, the chaotic gusts before a storm, and of course walking in the wind—with it, against it, carried by it—I love it all.

I was delighted to discover the Dutch have a word for spending time in the wind: *Uitwaaien*. It specifically involves going for a walk or bike ride in nature, particularly in windy conditions, to clear the mind and rejuvenate the body and spirit. It is an effective means of self-care and stress reduction that requires no equipment, just the cooperation of Mother Nature. According to Caitlin Meyer, quoted in *Nautilus* magazine, "Uitwaaien is something you do to clear your mind and feel refreshed—out with the bad air, in with the good ... It's seen as a pleasant, easy, and relaxing experience—a way to destress or escape from daily life."

"Who has seen the wind?
Neither you nor I.
But when the trees bow down their heads,
The wind is passing by."

Christina Rossetti, "Who Has Seen the Wind"

Weather Winds

Yet with all this thought about wind it occurred to me that, although I understood my *experience* of wind, I had little idea of what it actually is. According to *National Geographic*, "Wind is the movement of air, caused by the uneven heating of the Earth by the sun and the Earth's own rotation." So as our planet spins, heats, and cools, air is stirred and stilled.

Pay attention to the wind as you walk—it can give you many clues about other activity on the surface of the planet. These weather winds are adapted from Tristan Gooley's *The Lost Art of Reading Nature's Signs*.

- If the wind shifts—grows stronger or weaker or changes direction altogether—know that a change in weather is coming.
- If this shift in wind is markedly in a clockwise direction, the weather will likely get worse.
- The wind often picks up before a storm because rising air pressure creates a vacuum that the wind rushes in to fill. It often dies down after a storm because the falling air pressure behind the storm creates a high-pressure system that blocks the wind.
- Standing with your back to the wind, look upward and notice the highest clouds. As you do, recite this rhyme: *Left to right, not quite right.* If that is the direction in which they are moving the weather is about to turn—hopefully you have remembered your umbrella and galoshes.

Practice

Even on windless days you can blow the cobwebs out
of your mind with a wind visualization practice taught by
meditation teacher and psychologist Tara Brach in her book
Radical Acceptance. It is a type of meditation that involves
your imagination and goes something like this:

- Find a quiet place where you will not be disturbed.
  Imagine yourself standing in a field on a windy day or
  picture the wind as a flowing river or spiraling vortex.
- As you do, focus on the different qualities of wind, such
  as its temperature, power, and direction.
- Feel the wind blowing through your hair and clothes.
  See the trees swaying and the birds gliding on its currents.
  Listen to the sound of the wind rustling through the leaves.
- You might even want to free-associate words that speak
  to you of the wind—transform, cleanse, free, elevate ...
- Stay with this visualization for a few minutes, or as long as
  you like. Afterward, check in with yourself. Do you feel
  refreshed? Has bad air given way to fresh breezes?

Mushrooms and Fungi

When we walk in the woods or a forest, we see about a third of everything that lives there. We can't miss the trees, of course, but there are whole elements that go unseen, from microscopic bacteria, to insects, to camouflaged creatures and the mycelium— mushroom or fungi.

Autumn marks the end of the mushroom foraging season but there are few things that are best found as the summer's heat cools and before winter's frost. Oyster mushrooms do not start fruiting until temperatures fall and remain in the low 50°F (10°C). Puffballs, honey mushrooms, and hen-of-the-woods all like the cooler, wetter weather.

Fungi can give us a lot of information about the surrounding landscape that we're walking in:

- Fly agaric or amanita mushrooms, easily recognized by their red domes and white spots, almost always grow near birch trees. (Beware: although pretty they are also powerfully psychoactive.)
- Lilac milk caps grow near alder trees.
- Hen-of-the-woods favor oaks, especially rotting ones after a lightning strike.
- Golden chanterelles tend to grow under pines and other conifers.
- Parasol fungi grow in open meadows but tell us that there are woods nearby.
- Pine fire fungus and bonfire scaly cap crop up after a forest fire.
- Rooting poisonpie is aptly named since it grows over small animal remains.

"Fungi provide a key to understanding the planet on which we live, and the ways we think, feel, and behave ... The more we learn about fungi, the less makes sense without them."

Merlin Sheldrake, *Entangled Life*

The Wood Wide Web

Andrew Adamatzky, Professor in Unconventional
Computing at the University of the West of England,
used microelectrodes to better understand if fungi
communicate. He studied the electrical spikes given
off by four species of fungi—enoki, split gill, ghost, and
caterpillar. He discovered that these spikes were not
random and indeed seemed to work like language,
positing a vocabulary of about fifty "words." In the
Guardian, Adamatzky suggested that the electrical
activity is likely to, "maintain the fungi's integrity—
analogous to wolves howling to maintain the integrity
of the pack—or to report newly discovered sources of
attractants and repellents to other parts of their mycelia."

Yet the mushrooms are not just talking with each other. "Mycorrhiza" is the word for symbiotic relationship between fungi and the root system of vascular plants such as mosses, ferns, and trees, providing them with information and nutrients in exchange for carbohydrates. This interconnectedness of trees and other plants through underground fungal networks has been named the "wood wide web." I imagine the term is supposed to evoke the internet, but I like to picture it as intricate, softer, and more magical, a sparkling complex system of webs.

Yet as Merlin Sheldrake reminds us in his book *Entangled Life*, "The interconnectedness of fungi is not just metaphorical. It is literal. Fungal networks can stretch for miles, and they can connect thousands of individual organisms. These networks allow fungi to share resources, communicate with each other, and even coordinate their activities." The wood wide web allows trees to share resources like water, nutrients, and even carbon. This helps them to survive in harsh conditions and to recover from disturbances like drought and fire. It can send chemical signals to warn other trees other of danger such as pests or disease. It also allows them to form resilient communities, which means if one tree is damaged or destroyed, the others can help to support it.

Just as it gives rise to the lines demarcating sentience (the capacity of a being to experience feelings and sensations), the complex interactions within the wood wide web are an elegant metaphor for the interdependence and interconnectedness of all beings. It evokes awe and understanding of how nature is interrelated—nothing is an individual organism, but part of a larger community.

BEWARE ...

Please do not guess about which fungi you can eat! If you are walking into the world of mushroom gathering for the first time, go with an experienced and reputable forager. Eating the wrong mushroom can cause nausea, hallucinations, liver failure, or even death.

Labyrinths

Most of us live in a society so committed to "getting somewhere" it
can be really difficult to go nowhere. That is what makes walking a
labyrinth such a powerful practice.

There is a difference between labyrinths and mazes. Mazes have
many paths and dead ends, not all of which will get you to the middle.
Labyrinths have a single, continuous path leading to a center: they are
about the walking not arriving.

"The labyrinth is a metaphor for the journey of life ... a path of self-discovery, a journey into the center of our own hearts."

John Michell, *Sacred England*

Paths with Intention

Labyrinths symbolize the process of arriving at our own center. They have been used since ancient times for various purposes, including meditation, contemplation, and creating spiritual space. Labyrinths can be found in art and architecture from ancient Greece and Egypt, and in many medieval cathedrals, from Ireland to Nepal, perhaps most famously at Chartres in France.

All of these early labyrinth builders were onto something—nowadays labyrinths are being built and walked not just at sacred sites but at hospitals, hospices, and mental health centers.

Traveling step by step through a labyrinth can be a mindful and introspective experience. From a neurological perspective, it engages the brain's attentional processes, takes you out of "fight or flight," and contributes to a meditative state.

Most importantly, it evokes the relaxation response, which is characterized by a number of physiological changes, including decreased heart rate, blood pressure, and muscle tension, slowed breathing, and increased alpha brain waves (which occur when we're relaxed but not concentrating). The relaxation response also has significant long-term health benefits, including lowering blood pressure and breathing rates, reducing incidents of chronic pain and insomnia, and even improving fertility! Like many kinds of mediation practice it can lead to enhanced concentration, a sense of control and efficiency in one's life. All of this from such a simple practice!

TRY THIS ...

While raking fallen leaves in autumn, you can create your own labyrinth. It can be as complex as you like, or perhaps a simple circle. It will serve a dual purpose—a place to walk, a place for contemplation, and (when the first strong October winds gust) a lesson in impermanence.

Practice

The beauty of walking a labyrinth is that the path is set for you. There are no decisions to make, no directions to choose. Just one foot in front of the other. It is a self-directed process and can take minutes or even hours, it is all up to you. As you walk:

- Set an intention. What do you hope to gain as you amble through the labyrinth. Are you solving a problem or looking for peace? After you have set your intention, inhale and exhale a few times to ground yourself and begin walking.

- Be mindful. Pay attention to your breathing but also the sensations of your body. Notice your feet touching the ground, the sun, or rain on your skin, the sounds of birds ...

- Notice what sensations arise in your mind—judgment, impatience, doubt? Do your best to let go of these and stay with the embodied meditation of walking the labyrinth.

- Some people like to visualize as they engage in the walking process. Perhaps you will imagine walking through obstacles—things or people that have been holding you back from a dream or desire. Or you might picture yourself in a garden, the woods, or a churchyard, even if you are not in one. You might choose to listen to a beloved teacher or your own inner voice, offering insight, guidance, and wisdom ... perhaps even an epiphany.

- As you arrive at the labyrinth's center, pause. Be where you are and take a moment to say thank you to all the conditions that gave you the opportunity for this practice. Say a little prayer, whisper, "Thank you" to the wind, or simply clear your mind and see what arises.

After you have completed your labyrinth walk, assess the experience. How do you feel? What insights did you receive?

Memory: Attention and Return

So many times, I will find myself trying to recall an idea, grasping for an answer, and be unable to capture it ... until I go for a walk. Then (usually when I've left pen and paper behind), all is revealed! It turns out such epiphanies are not just my experience—walking and memory are thoroughly entangled.

Walking increases blood flow to the brain, helping to deliver oxygen and nutrients to the cells. It also releases endorphins—the "feel good" hormones—which can have mood-boosting effects. Because walking can help to reduce stress and anxiety, it can clear the mind, increasing our focus and contributing to the act of remembering. It even has a direct physical effect—increasing the size of the hippocampus, the part of the brain involved in memory and learning.

Not only can walking improve and sustain your memory; it can help to unlock old memories too. Walking through places we used to frequent can stir up recollections and open a floodgate of feelings. Meandering through old neighborhoods can trigger nostalgia, reminding us of old homes, friends, school, and all the experiences that went with them. These can be sparked by the sights, sounds, smells, and even the feel of the ground beneath our feet. This happens for a few reasons, but primarily because neural pathways are re-activated, stirring up the original experience in our brains. Reflecting on what we recall from our personal history can help us to understand our past and appreciate our present.

In his novel *Slowness*, Milan Kundera wrote, "There is a secret bond between slowness and memory, between speed and forgetting." It is a lesson that we can all apply to our lives. As you walk, slow your pace, pay attention, and be where you are, not where you are going.

"Stretches of path can carry
memories of a person, just as
a person might of a path."

Robert MacFarlane, *The Old Ways*

CHAPTER 4

A Winter Walk ...

Sometimes a winter walk is about what is no longer there—birds, flowers, leaves, and sunshine. But with this absence comes more opportunity to pay attention to what *is* there. Empty bird nests are visible, trees take on new forms, revealing their skeletal structure, the north wind shifts from dynamic to ferocious, and of course, snow can descend with a whisper or a clumpy onslaught. Frost paints surfaces with its fractal patterns, and ever-optimistic squirrels and chipmunks grow less timid in hopes of a handout.

Seneca the Younger wrote "All that begins also ends" and winter walks contain beginnings within the endings. Under the slush, frost, and ice, await the first tendrils and promises of spring, and we know that dark days will eventually surrender to the return of light.

The Menace and the Marvels of Ice

Take a moment to think about ice. Isn't it amazing? A liquid becomes a solid that can return to liquid and the cycle can repeat again and again. Such a nice metaphor for transformation and impermanence.

Ice is the solid state of water, typically formed at or below temperatures of 32°F (0°C). When moisture in the air meets these conditions, ice crystals form and it falls from the sky as snow. Walking in the snow—at least for me having grown up in the Midwestern United States—is such a thrill, no matter how many times I do it. Especially new snowfall—the fluff, the crunch, the slog, is a sensory experience like no other. Sound is different after a snowfall, absorbed and muffled, offering up a unique kind of silence—even birds and traffic are hushed. Because snow is such a good insulator it can make walking outdoors invigorating, letting you know where your edges are (especially if you are dressed for the occasion). The smell is the qualia of crisp and blue. And then there is the light—the morning sun sparkling on the snow and fading into eerie blue on a moonlit night. It is all magic as far as I am concerned.

"When we stride or stroll across the frozen lake,
We place our feet where they have never been.
We walk upon the unwalked."

Robert Bly, "Gratitude to Old Teachers"

If you feel yourself losing your balance, bend your knees and lower your center of gravity. Or try out a pair of walking sticks, ice cleats, or even snowshoes.

The Language of Snow

The Indigenous peoples of Alaska, Canada, and Siberia have inhabited the vast Arctic regions of North America for generations and are adept at communicating in snowy conditions and landscapes. A stone landmark called an inuksuk (see above) is used by Inuit and other Indigenous peoples to guide travelers, warn of danger, assist hunters, or mark places of reverence.

There is a cliché (actually, a myth) that the Indigenous peoples have fifty words for snow. Scholars, beginning with anthropologist Franz Boaz in the 1880s, have deliberated on this, and although it is not exactly the case, the Inuit language and related dialects have myriad words

that evoke snow and ice, some poems unto themselves. The Eskimo language describes ice with poetic clarity and precision:

- Freshwater ice, for drinking
- The first layer of thin ice formed on puddles in autumn
- New ice appearing on the sea or on rock surfaces
- Ice that looks like windows
- Ice that breaks after being tested with a harpoon
- Ice that has cracked because of tide changes, which has refrozen
- Slushy ice by the sea

All these words remind us that there are so many levels of perception. Just as we can walk the same path many times and have a new experience or realization each time, so we can look at the same thing—be it snow or ice—and come to it in a whole new way.

Practice

Try listening to ice after a snowstorm—the crackle, the drip, the silence. And if you are snowed in and housebound, there is a simple meditation practice that you can do indoors. Place an ice cube on a dish. Sit still, and in a comfortable position nearby, watch the ice cube melt. Every time your mind strays, return your attention to the process of ice returning to water.

Being Cold: Finding Your Edge

I love going for walks on crisp, cold days because it reminds me where my edges are. There is a physical sensation of "me" and "weather" that is not experienced in quite the same way during more clement times. Likewise, walking in winter is usually more challenging, bringing us not just to a temperature "edge" but to the edge of our physical ability. It is in those edges where growth comes—not only in terms of stamina, but in our understanding of our place as we move through the world.

TRY THIS ...

Even (or perhaps especially) when it is cold outside, go for a walk! And try to do it when the sun is shining brightest. Not only is this likely be the easiest time of day for a trek, but you will benefit from a dose of vitamin D. Among its many benefits, this "sunshine vitamin" can strengthen the immune system and boost your mood, which so many of us become deficient in during the winter. Of course, where you walk matters. If you live in a climate like Boston, Massachusetts, in the US, you will need to spend 23 minutes outside at noon to produce enough vitamin D for the day.

Cold exposure, such as ice baths and cold showers, is on trend these days—and there is a reason for it, as the physiological and psychological benefits are many. As well as improving circulation, exposure to cold temperatures can activate the body's stress response, triggering the release of happy endorphins, and increasing feelings of wellbeing and even euphoria. The act of pushing one's boundaries past chilly to cold may have psychological implications in terms of developing resilience and faith in one's abilities. It all sounds good on paper, but despite all the scientific studies I've read, I'd much rather take a walk in the cold than a dip in ice water.

According to a study published in the *American Journal of Human Biology*, we burn 34 percent more calories when we hike in cold weather than in more clement conditions. It makes intuitive sense—the physical exertion of tromping through snow or navigating ice is combined with the energy it takes to stay warm. And walking in cold air is by its nature invigorating and energizing, which means (if we do not get too cold) we are able to sustain a brisk pace for longer than we can on a hot summer's day.

"The edge is not a place in space,
it is a place in the mind."

Bruce Lee

Practice

The Discourse on the Foundations of Mindfulness is a core Buddhist meditation practice that is said to cultivate awareness and compassion. The foundations are comprised of four parts:

- Mindfulness of Body: paying attention to physical sensations, without getting caught up in analyses or judgment.
- Mindfulness of Feelings: paying attention to all our feelings— whether unpleasant, neutral, or pleasant—by allowing instead of pushing away.
- Mindfulness of the Mind: paying attention to our thoughts and emotions, simply noticing them without suppressing or obsessing.
- Mindfulness of Dhammas: also known as the nature of reality or the way things are. This involves paying attention to the phenomenal world (the world as it appears, and is understood by, humans). As with body, feelings, and mind, we notice, acknowledge, and—like watching clouds in a winter sky—let our observations drift away.

Now, take this ancient practice, which can be adapted to any belief system, and apply it to walking in the cold.

- The first part is quite easy—pay attention to the cold on your skin, from your forehead to your toes. Where do you end and the weather begin? Where is the edge?
- As you walk, examine your feelings. Do you want to get this over with? Are you easing into it? Does it make you feel good?
- What is going on in your mind? By becoming mindful of your body and feelings, have you given more space to thoughts and emotions? Examine them and, like ice melting, let them glide away.
- Once you are in a space where your feelings and mind are opened and clear, what happens? Do you feel more connected to the world around you? More able to be present? To just ... be?

Kinhin: Meditation in Motion

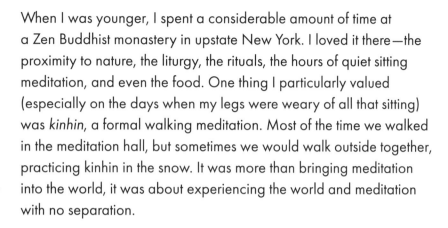

When I was younger, I spent a considerable amount of time at a Zen Buddhist monastery in upstate New York. I loved it there—the proximity to nature, the liturgy, the rituals, the hours of quiet sitting meditation, and even the food. One thing I particularly valued (especially on the days when my legs were weary of all that sitting) was *kinhin*, a formal walking meditation. Most of the time we walked in the meditation hall, but sometimes we would walk outside together, practicing kinhin in the snow. It was more than bringing meditation into the world, it was about experiencing the world and meditation with no separation.

All walking is a meditation of sorts, but kinhin follows a specific path. As meditation teacher Jan Chozen Bays wrote in *How to Train a Wild Elephant*, "Silent walking is a bridge between one side of meditation—silent sitting in pure awareness—and the other side—speaking and moving about."

Kinhin is, of course, about attention, but it is also about slowing down—truly slowing down, which is not as easy as you might think. Here is how to do it:

1 Find a location to walk without distractions. It should be a place where you will not draw attention to yourself, especially if you are outdoors. Make sure the path you have chosen is fairly easy, so that you can focus on just walking, not navigation.

2 Lower your gaze, but do not be inattentive, especially when you are walking outdoors.

3 Become conscious of your breath (but do not control it) as you begin walking slowly—very slowly—and deliberately. Notice the rise and fall of your chest, and the feeling of the air as it enters and leaves your lungs. Perhaps it slows to the point of synchronizing with your steps.

4 Feel the entire motion of your footfall, from heel touching ground to toe rising, as your weight shifts. Then the next step, and the next.

5 Your pace should be slow enough that you can remain aware of each step and breath. Now, move even more slowly ...

6 Be aware of your body. As you walk, pay attention to your posture and your body's alignment. Keep your back straight and your shoulders relaxed. All the while, notice the sensations in your feet as they contact the ground and your breath in unison.

7 Let go of thoughts. Use the process of walking and breathing to keep you connected to the present moment.

8 Be compassionate and patient with yourself. Your mind will wander, and when it does, gently bring it back to your breath or your body. There is no need to judge yourself or get frustrated. You will find that this practice will allow you to gradually develop the ability to stay in the present moment for longer periods of time.

9 After walking for a while at the slowest pace possible, you can adjust your speed to fit your level of comfort. Zen kinhin usually begins almost impossibly slowly (especially if you are a city dweller who is used to walking fast) and then can pick up to a comfortable, brisk, or even fast pace. I once visited a monastery where the walking meditation became running, which was exhilarating but also a challenge—I wonder where my "presence" was then?

10 There is no set time for kinhin, which is another reason why it is easy adapt to walking outdoors, even in winter. You can practice for as long as you like.

TRY THIS ...

When practicing this walking meditation, do not swing your arms or put your hands in your pockets. There is a reason why Zen Buddhist monks walk with their hands clasped in front of them in *gassho* (prayer position) or in *shashu* (right hand over left fist)—it helps to create stillness of the body, which offers stillness of the mind.

Clear Skies, Moon Phases, and Starlight

In winter the sky is more discernable—this is the gift the trees give between releasing their leaves and budding again. The planets and stars seem closer, more visible. The winter nights are longer, giving us more time to observe the heavenly bodies as they move through the sky. All of these are reasons why winter can be the best time for a stargazing walk.

Winter nights tend to be clearer than summer nights. Cold air is denser than warm air, so it does not hold as much moisture, and less vapor means less haze and fewer clouds. On clear, cold nights, especially if you can find a place free of urban light pollution, it is possible to see about 3,000 stars with the naked eye, even some of the most distant and faintest stars in the night sky. So, while you are walking, look up!

For me, of all the lights in the sky, no matter the season, the moon is the most captivating. This winter moon has inspired names that feel like poetry: The Cold Moon because it occurs during the coldest time of year in the Northern Hemisphere. The Hunger Moon because it occurs during a time when animals are hibernating, and plants are scarce. And my favorite, Cheechakon, a name given by Native American Algonquins, which means "the moon when the geese return." Yet no matter the label, the winter moon is often seen as a symbol of hope and renewal. It marks the end of winter and start of a new lunar cycle, as spring can be glimpsed just over the horizon.

"The winter night sky was a reminder of our smallness in the universe, and our connection to something greater than ourselves."

Ishmael Reed, *Mumbo Jumbo*

The Power of Pausing

Even though it seems intuitive to take a break from walking—whether a park bench, a cozy café, or a spot on a trail with a beautiful view—resting is something I am not particularly good at, even when hiking. I tend to have two gears: "Let's go!" and "I'm exhausted."

I've found that mindfulness, or any sort of attention or meditation practice, can really help with this. It took me a long time to believe that people who took breaks and got a sensible eight-ish hours of sleep were not lacking in energy, but the opposite—restoring and distributing energy instead of depleting themselves. Now that I've discovered napping, especially in winter, it has become one of my favorite things—I will never turn back.

"Resting in winter is a way of honoring the natural rhythms of the earth. When we rest, we are in sync with the seasons and with the cycles of life."

Tricia Hersey, The Nap Ministry

During the darker winter months, many of us suffer from SAD (seasonal affective disorder). The lack of natural sunlight affects our sleep patterns and overall energy levels, which can lead to depression, sleepless fatigue, decreased motivation, and changes in appetite or sleep patterns. So, whenever you have access to natural light—even through a window—take a sun bath, ideally exposing your uncovered skin to the healing rays.

Winter's Natural Sleep Aid

Cold weather is a natural sleep aid in many ways. Not only because the nights are longer and darker and our beds somehow cozier, but because cold exposure during the day can improve the quality of our sleep at night, especially as we get older. Scientists from Tohoku Fukushi University monitored those who were exposed to a cold or cool environment—around 55°F (13°C)—for an hour before bedtime and measured their sleep. The results showed that exposure to cold was associated with an increase in slow-wave sleep (our deepest sleep state) and a decrease in wakefulness after falling asleep.

Long winter nights help us sleep in other ways as well. In winter we produce more melatonin (the hormone that helps to regulate sleep–wake cycles). This signals to the body that it is time to conserve energy, and so promotes sleep.

If cold weather can improve our sleep, then walking in winter can improve it even more. According to psychologists from Brandeis University, walking can have a marked effect on how long and well we sleep. When they focused on people like those with insomnia, residents of nursing homes, those with depression, cancer, and Alzheimer's disease, and women transitioning through menopause, they found a direct correlation between walking and improved sleep efficiency. Participants showed reduced nighttime wakefulness and next-day fatigue, as well as a decrease in depressive symptoms. A more general study found that people who walked for 30 minutes in cold weather, five days a week for a month had improved sleep quality compared to those who did not. So, even on the coldest days, bundle up, put on sturdy boots, and go for a walk—especially if you are having trouble sleeping.

Practice

So often we are in a hurry to get out of the cold, but when you are able, take a moment to pause and be *with* the cold. Try to give the sensation as much attention and appreciation as you would summer sunlight on your skin or a fragrant spring breeze. There is a benefit—an energetic stillness—in being with cold that is so easy to miss. Allow yourself to savor it.

Breath Made Visible

When breathing outdoors during the winter—inhaling cold air and exhaling clouds—we are reminded that our breath is not merely an idea or concept, but physical—made up of gases and vapor.

When it comes to making our breath visible, it is the vapor that is key. Our bodies are composed of almost 70 percent water and the air in our lungs is saturated with water vapor, which is at the same temperature as our bodies 98.6°F (37°C). Cold air does not retain as much moisture as warm air, so when we exhale on a winter's day, the heat of our breath meets the chill air and, for a moment, reaches dew point (the temperature that creates condensation). This forms the droplets of water that create ephemeral, misty clouds.

Seeing our breath makes us more conscious of the many ways that breathing is a spiritual experience—from watching a newborn baby gulp their first lungful or air to holding the hand of a loved one as they exhale their last. It seems apt that the word "spiritual" is derived from the ecclesiastical Latin, *spiritualis*, which means not only "pertaining to spirit" but interestingly "of or pertaining to breath, breathing, wind, or air."

Practice

A lovely way to pay attention to the breath and "meditate in motion" on winter days is by taking up a practice called chi walking. Start by standing with your feet shoulder width apart and your arms relaxed at your sides. Take a few deep breaths and focus on your body. As you exhale, begin to walk slowly, taking long, conscious, deliberate steps.

As you walk, imagine that you are sending energy (chi) from your feet into the ground, creating an energetic connection and cycle. Visualize chi as breath when it has condensed into clouds, surging and wafting through your body, from your nose as you inhale to the soles of your feet.

This Hush of Nature

If I had to pick but one religion, I would say I am devoted to what poet Samuel Taylor Coleridge called "this hush of nature." After air, water, and food (and maybe books), quiet—especially the quiet of the outdoors—is essential to me. I aspire to times when the world is as still as glaciers melting.

I have been on a lifelong quest to find the quietest time of day to walk, and I have not yet discovered the answer. Based on my regular walk around New York Harbor, I would guess it is early in the morning—just as dawn is breaking, as the mist is rising off the water, before the light snow has been trampled by humans or scampered in by dogs. Of course, there are sounds then too, like goose squawk and buoy bells, or wind in the branches, yet somehow these seem to enhance the quiet instead of detracting from it.

"They walked in the snow, their feet sinking silently into the soft whiteness ... The silence was so deep that it seemed to envelop them, shutting them off from the rest of the world."

Zora Neale Hurston, *Their Eyes Were Watching God*

TRY THIS ...

In his book, *In Praise of Walking*, Thomas A. Clark wrote, "When I spend a day talking I feel exhausted, when I spend it walking I am pleasantly tired." The next time you walk, deliberately eliminate noise and listen to the silence! Leave your earbuds, to-do list, and (if you dare!) your phone behind. Consider your attention levels as you walk and how, when you are chatting or listening to chatter, it is pretty much impossible to be fully present.

Sacred Silence

Every religion takes up silent practice in one way or another. Buddhists meditate for days—even years—without speaking, to become better attuned to the true nature of reality. Benedictine and Trappist Christians hold silence in high regard as a way of shunning distraction and paying attention to God. And most people "need a little quiet" at one point or another. Unsurprisingly, there are physical and psychological benefits to turning down the volume: it improves focus and concentration, diminishes stress, and boosts creativity as the quiet allows buried or subconscious thoughts to emerge.

It is not just humans who benefit from silence, but the natural world too. It is easy to understand how loud sounds—like fireworks, ATVs, and leaf blowers—can impact animals. Even loud conversation in less-populated areas of a park or on a trail can scare them from their hive or

Practice

I am a great admirer of environmentalist John Francis, also known as "The Planet Walker", who spent 17 years—from 1973 to 1990—in silence as he walked across the entire, contiguous 48 states of the US and South America. His message of respect for the Earth is important, but we do not have to go to quite such extremes. Consider taking up your own silent, walking practice. Make it more than an experiment—imbue it with ritual by walking for an hour or even half an hour each week without speaking. What do you hear around you? What do you hear from within?

burrow, mask the sound of the predators, or interfere with communication, especially during mating periods.

Karen Armstrong wrote in *Sacred Nature*, "To glimpse the sacrality of the natural world requires a degree of quiet and solitude that is hard to come by today. Indeed, we seem to find silence alien and often deliberately eliminate it from our lives." That is why I was delighted to discover there is a whole travel industry that has grown up around silence. In Lapland, Finland, and many other countries around the world, foundations like Quiet Parks International have formed. They are "committed to saving quiet for the benefit of all life" and seek to preserve quiet, not just in the wilderness, but in urban spaces as well. It makes me wonder about those who have never experienced true silence and it is exciting to me that there are people dedicating to providing the opportunity.

"We're all just walking each other home"

Ram Dass's often-quoted words, "We're all just walking each other home" are especially meaningful as we walk with the seasons—taking a path of interconnection to arrive together at a place of wholeness, community, and interconnection with nature and our true selves.

Yet, there is no end to this path. Nature does not work that way, and neither does life. Everything is a cycle of departure and return, blooming and dying, and blooming again. Noting in nature remains in one place. Even mountains move, swaying with seismic shift, albeit very slowly.

We see it in the seasons, of course—the moment when we sense spring rain tinged with summer's warmth, the breeze of autumn blowing us through to winter's freeze, the knowledge that under slush, snow, and ice is a promise of incubating bulbs and seeds. In winter, not only do new leaves and fruit await in trees, but so do dormant larvae, some spiders, and even bees. Snakes and lizards enter brumation, a torpor that is not quite as deep as hibernation.

Departure and Return

Animals retreat into their burrows in winter, so there are fewer creatures to see as we walk. Although we may notice more empty nests in the bare trees, the birds are still busy. Seagulls battle for whatever they can scavenge, songbirds linger and tussle at feeders, and if you are lucky, you will spot a snow goose or gannet. Many are just here for the winter—the communities of birds and

"The four elements return to their nature as a child to its mother."

The Heart Sutra

geese shift, some shorebirds moving a short distance inland, others migrating great ways like Arctic terns, who fly a 44,000-mile (70,811km) route from the Arctic to Antarctica.

The entire cycle of migration is miraculous, particularly the way terns, not to mention geese, swans, cranes, and hummingbirds, know their proper timing and route. Some of it is instinctual, but much of it is learned from their parents and imprinted after their first migration. Changing light levels—the diminishing winter sunlight and increasing hours in spring—provide cues as does the angle of the sun. Some birds even have chemicals in their brain, eyes, or beaks that function like internal compasses, allowing them to sense Earth's magnetic field. And many of them pay attention (as should we when we are walking!) to the geography—mountain ranges and coastlines as well as specific constellations—as they travel the same route year after year.

Practice

Meditation teachers often offer the phrase: simply begin again. Apply this to your walks, no matter the season. Think about walking as worship, ritual, or sacrament, not walking for the sake of walking. Doesn't each stroll end with some kind of homecoming?

Butterflies too, have an internal compass to orient themselves, which senses the Earth's magnetic field and tracks the sun. Monarch butterflies follow the scent of milkweed plants—their only food source—which draws them to their winter homes in the mountain forests of Mexico where they wait until spring to begin the migration route again.

This cycle of departure and return is mirrored by the moon in twenty-eight days as it waxes to full, then wanes to new, pulling the tides from flood to ebb.

There are human cycles of rebirth and repetition, too—planting time, harvest time, New Year celebrations, summer vacation, return to school in the autumn. Even the youngest children know some of the markers and symbols, like March kites and October pumpkins. Although we use them to organize our human lives, our divisions of days, months, and years have their natural origins in astronomical observations. I suppose we have always wanted to see the patterns and cycles around us and connect with them in a primordial way.

"Earth may be ... alive like a tree. A tree that quietly exists, never moving except to sway in the wind, yet endlessly conversing with the sunlight and the soil."

James Lovelock, *Gaia*

Bibliography

American Natural History Museum "The Science behind Singing Mice and Laughing Rats" (December, 2017) www.amnh.org/explore/news-blogs/news-posts/the-science-behind-singing-mice-and-laughing-rats

Anderson, Eileen "How Does Dogs' Hearing Compare to Humans'?" *Eileen and Dogs* (2019). eileenanddogs.com/blog/2019/03/21/dogs-hearing-vs-human-hearing/

Armstrong, Karen *Sacred Nature: Restoring Our Ancient Bond with the Natural World* (Knopf Doubleday Publishing Group, 2022)

Ask the Doctors "How much sunshine do I need for enough Vitamin D?" UCLA Health. www.uclahealth.org/news/ask-the-doctors-round-sun-exposure-vital-to-vitamin-d-production

Bays, Jan Chozen *How to Train a Wild Elephant: And Other Adventures in Mindfulness* (Shambhala, 2011)

Bodhi, Bikkhu "The Buddha's Four Foundations of Mindfulness" (*Lion's Roar*, January, 2023)

Bolz-Weber, Nadia *Accidental Saints: Finding God in All the Wrong People* (HarperOne, 2014)

Brach, Tara *Radical Acceptance: Embracing Your Life With the Heart of a Buddha* (Bantam Books, 2003)

Brown, Kimberly *Navigating Grief and Loss: 25 Buddhist Practices to Keep Your Heart Open to Yourself and Others* (Prometheus Books, 2022)

"Buddhist Circumambulation" *Tricycle* (The Buddhist Review, 2019) tricycle.org/beginners/buddhism/buddhist-circumambulation/

Buswell, Robert E., & Lopez, D. S. *The Princeton Dictionary of Buddhism* (Princeton University Press, 2014)

Carson, Jacob R. et al. "Neighborhood walkability, neighborhood social health, and self-selection among U.S. adults." *Health & Place* 82 (2023): 103036

Chan A.W. et al. "Evaluation of the Effectiveness of Tai Chi versus Brisk Walking." *International Journal of Environmental Research and Public Health*, 2016 Jul 5;13(7):682

Cho, Kyoung Sang et al. "Terpenes from Forests and Human Health." *Toxicological Research* 33, 2 (2017): 97-106

Chödrön, Pema *When Things Fall Apart: Heart Advice for Difficult Times* (Shambhala, 2000)

Cimpean, Alina, et al. "The Impact of Walking on Mental Health: A Systematic Review and Meta-Analysis." *Journal of Affective Disorders* 241, no. 1, (2019): 13–29

Coutty, Tom "In Which Country Do People Walk the Most?" *The Circular* (May, 2022)

Coverley, Merlin *The Art of Wandering: The Writer as Walker* (Oldcastle Books, 2012)

Cropper, Simon J., Hamacher, Duane. W., & Little, Daniel. R. "Why People Across the World See Constellations, Not Just Stars." *Psyche* (August, 2022)

Dana, William Starr *How to Know the Wild Flowers* (Dover, 1963)

del Pozo Cruz B, Ahmadi MN, Lee I, Stamatakis E. "Prospective Associations of Daily Step Counts and Intensity with Cancer and Cardiovascular Disease Incidence ..." *JAMA Internal Medicine* 182, no. 11 (2022): 1139–1148

De Vries, Saskia, et al. "Walking in Nature: Effects on Mood, Cognition, and Stress." *Frontiers in Psychology*, 16 (2015): 1098

Douglas Harper Online Etymology Dictionary. (2023). www.etymonline.com/

Dreyer, Danny *ChiWalking: Fitness Walking for Lifelong Health and Energy* (Atria, 2006)

Dungy, Camille T. *Black Nature: Four Centuries of African American Nature Poetry* (The University of Georgia Press, 2009)

Elgin, Dag. T. "Henrik Ibsen's Use of 'Friluftsliv'." (2009). norwegianjournaloffriluftsliv.com/doc/ibsens_use_of_friluftsliv_elgvin_2009.pdf

EPA. "What if We Kept Our Cars Parked for Trips Less than One Mile?" U.S. Environmental Protection Agency, 2018. www.epa.gov/greenvehicles/what-if-we-kept-our-cars-parked-trips-less-one-mile

"Fall Wind" American Meteorological Society, (2023). glossary.ametsoc.org/wiki/Fall_wind

Field, T. "The Benefits of Chi Walking." *American Journal of Preventive Medicine* 28, no. 2 (2005): 141–144

Fleerackers, Alice "The Simple Dutch Cure for Stress" *Nautilus* (November, 2019). nautil.us/the-simple-dutch-cure-for-stress-8594/

Fleming, Amy "Let There Be Light! Why Sunny Spring Days Make Us Happier and Healthier" *The Guardian* (May, 2021)

Georgiou, Michail, Gordon Morison, Niamh Smith, Zoë Tieges, and Sebastien Chastin "Mechanisms of Impact of Blue Spaces on Human Health: A Systematic Literature Review and Meta-Analysis" *International Journal of Environmental Research and Public Health* 18, no. 5 (2021): 2486

Gibb, Charlotte "Human Nature." *The Psychologist* 33, no. 9 (2020): 704–707

Giles, Herbert A. *Chuang Tzu: Mystic, Moralist, and Social Reformer* (Bernard Quaritch, 1889)

Gooley, Tristan *The Lost Art of Reading Nature's Signs: Use Outdoor Clues to Find Your Way, Predict the Weather, Locate Water, Track Animals – and Other Forgotten Skills* (The Experiment, 2015)

"Green and Blue Spaces Together Provide Even Bigger Boost to Mental Health" (2023) studyfinds.org/walking-along-water-mental-health/

Hackensack Meridian Health "Walking to Remember" *Newswise* (May, 2023). www.newswise.com/articles/walking-to-remember

Han, Su-xia et al. "Serum dickkopf-1 is a novel serological biomarker for the diagnosis and prognosis of pancreatic cancer" *Oncotarget* 6, no. 23 (2015): 19907–19917

Haskell, David George *Thirteen Ways to Smell a Tree* (Octopus Publishing Group, 2022)

Heim, Maria *Words for the Heart: A Treasury of Emotions from Classical India* (Princeton University Press, 2022)

Horowitz, Alexandra *Inside of a Dog: What Dogs See, Smell, and Know* (Simon & Schuster, 2009)

Hurston, Zora Neale *Their Eyes Were Watching God* (Harper Perennial, 1998)

"Inuktitut Words for Snow and Ice" *The Canadian Encyclopedia. Historica Canada.* Article published July 08, 2015; Last Edited July 09, 2015

Ishimure, Michiko "Pure Land, Poisoned Sea" *Japan Quarterly* 3, no. 8 (1971): 300–306

Jackson-Grossblat, A., Carbonell, N., & Waite, D. "The Therapeutic Effects Upon Dog Owners Who Interact with Their Dogs in a Mindful Way" *Journal of Humanistic Psychology* 56, no. 2 (2016): 144–170

Jain, Shamini *Healing Ourselves: Biofield Science and the Future of Health* (Sounds True, 2021)

Journey North "Reasons for Seasons Teacher's Background Information." journeynorth.org/tm/mclass/ReasonsBack.html

Kabat-Zinn, Jon *Falling Awake: How to Practice Mindfulness in Everyday Life* (Hachette Books, 2018)

Kagge, Erling *Walking: One Step at a Time.* (Pantheon, 2019)

Kim, Dakota "For First Black Man to Wear Hiking's 'Triple Crown,' the Trails Are a Place for Healing." *LA Times* (February, 2023)

Kreiczer, Sarah "The Role of Mindfulness in Grief and Loss." *PMC*, 2023, 6801055. doi:10.1371/journal.pone.06801055

Kreiczer, Sarah "The Benefits of Mindfulness-Based Interventions for Grief and Loss." *PMC*, 2019, 4378297. doi:10.1371/journal.pone.04378297

Krisnamurti "Series I – Chapter 41 – 'Awareness". www.jkrishnamurti.org/content/series-i-chapter-41-awareness

LaMotte, Sandee "What's the Magic Number of Steps to Keep Weight Off? Here's What We Know" *CNN* (February, 2023)

"Leave No Trace Language Timeline" Green Mountain Club. www.greenmountainclub.org/leave-no-trace-language-timeline/

Ledesma, Carlos A., & Alan Teo "The Effects of Mindfulness-Based Interventions on Emotional Regulation and Psychological Well-Being: A Meta-Analysis " *Clinical Psychology Review* 34, no. 1 (2014): 1–12

Lewis, John *Walking with the Wind: A Memoir of the Movement* (Harvest Books, 1999)

Library of Congress "Why Do I See My Breath When It's Cold Outside?" (2023). www.loc.gov/everyday-mysteries/meteorology-climatology/item/why-do-i-see-my-breath-when-its-cold-outside/

Lovelock, James *Healing Gaia: Practical Medicine for the Planet* (Harmony Books, 1991)

Merriam-Webster.com (2023). www.merriam-webster.com

Michell, John *Sacred England* (Gothic Image Publications, 1996)

Millay, Edna St. Vincent *Into the World's Great Heart: Selected Letters of Edna St. Vincent Millay* (Yale University Press, 2023)

Moss, Chris "You'll Never Walk Alone: 10 Great UK Walking Festivals for Spring and Summer" *The Guardian* (May, 2023)

Natarajan, Janeni et al. "Poly(ester amide)s from Soybean Oil for Modulated Release and Bone Regeneration." *ACS applied materials & interfaces* 8, no. 38, (2016): 25170–84

"Neuroscience News" "Possible 'Steps' to Revealing Super-Agers" (April, 2023). neurosciencenews.com/walking-cognition-aging-23036/

Newport, Cal *Digital Minimalism: Choosing a Focused Life in a Noisy World* (Portfolio, 2019)

Nicholson, Nigel "How Hardwired Is Human Behavior?" *Harvard Business Review* (July-August 1998)

Norton , Jim "Britons Walked 1,588 Miles on Average This Year, Report Reveals." *Daily Mail Online* (December, 2022)

Okamoto-Mizuno, K., Mizuno, K. "Effects of thermal environment on sleep and circadian rhythm" *Journal of Physiological Anthropology* 31, 14 (2012)

Oppezzo, Marily, and Daniel L. Schwartz "Give Your Ideas Some Legs: The Positive Effect of Walking on Creative Thinking." *Journal of Experimental Psychology: Learning, Memory, and Cognition. American Psychological Association* (APA), 2014

Pollen Nation "Beetles" (2023). ucanr.edu/sites/PollenNation/Meet_The_Pollinators/Beetles/

Quiet Parks International "Quiet Parks" (2023) www.quietparks.org/

Robertson, Sarah, & Phoenix, Kaitlyn "These Winter Walking Tips Will Help You Stay Fit During the Colder Months." *Prevention* (October, 2020)

Salzberg, Sharon *Real Happiness* (Workman Publishing Company, 2019)

Shaw, Chloe *What Is a Dog?* (Flatiron Books, 2021)

Sheldrake, Merlin *Entangled Life: How Mushrooms Think, Sentient Plants, and the Secret Language of the Forest* (Penguin Random House, 2020)

Sheldrake, Rupert *Science and Spiritual Practices* (Counterpoint, 2018)

Shirane, Haruo *Japan and the Culture of the Four Seasons* (Columbia University Press, 2012)

Sima, Richard "Birds' Song and Nature's Mental Health Benefits." *The Washington Post* (2023)

Singleton, Aled M. "Walking Is a State of Mind – It can Teach You So Much About Where You Are." *The Conversation* (May, 2022).

Solnit, Rebecca *A Field Guide to Getting Lost* (Penguin Books, 2006)

Song, Chorong, Harumi Ikei, and Yoshifumi Miyazaki "Seasonal Differences in Physiological Responses to Walking in Urban Parks" *International Journal of Environmental Research and Public Health* 19, no. 19 (2022): 12154.

Song, C., Ikei, H., Igarashi, M., Miwa, M., Takagaki, M., & Miyazaki, Y. "Physiological and psychological responses of young males during spring-time walks in urban parks." *Journal of Physiological Anthropology* 33, no. 8 (2014).

Suler, Asia *Mirrors in the Earth: Reflections on Self-Healing from the Living World* (North Atlantic Books, 2022)

Sullivan Bisson, Alycia N et al. "Walk to a better night of sleep: testing the relationship between physical activity and sleep" *Sleep Health* 5, 5 (2019): 487–494

The Atlantic "Walking" (2023) www.theatlantic.com/magazine/archive/1862/06/walking/304674/

"The Labyrinth Project." University of Massachusetts Dartmouth (February, 2023)

U.S. Department of Health and Human Services "Loneliness and Isolation" (May, 2023)

U.S. Forest Service "Scent" (2023)

Vancampfort, Davy, et al. "The Effect of Physical Activity on Anxiety and Depression in Adults: A Systematic Review and Meta-Analysis of Randomised Controlled Trials." *The Lancet Psychiatry* 3, no. 7 (2016): 650–661

"Walking and Mental Health." National Institute of Mental Health, U.S. Department of Health and Human Services (2022)

"Walking as Transportation: Benefits and Barriers." Centers for Disease Control and Prevention, U.S. Department of Health and Human Services (2022)

"Walking and Mental Health." National Institute of Mental Health, U.S. Department of Health and Human Services (2022)

Wexler, A. "A Theory for Living: Walking with Reggio Emilia." *Art Education* 57, no. 6 (2004): 13–19.

Whitman, Walt *Leaves of Grass* (Bantam Books, 2004)

Wohlleben, Peter *The Weather Detective: Rediscovering Nature's Secret Signs* (Dutton, 2018)

Woodbury, Anthony C. "Counting Eskimo Words for Snow: A Citizen's Guide" (1991). www.princeton.edu/~browning/snow.html

Whyte, David *The Heart Aroused: Poetry and the Preservation of the Soul in Corporate America* (HarperCollins, 1994)

Zhang, Y., Zhang, X., & Lu, Y. "The effects of chi walking on dopamine levels in healthy adults: A randomized controlled trial." *Journal of Alternative and Complementary Medicine* 21, no. 1 (2015): 33–38

Index

Acknowledgments

Gratitude to all the wise and patient folks at Ryland Peters & Small especially Kristine Pidkameny (this is book number eight or six depending on how you do the math!) along with Kristy Richardson, Penny Craig, and Carmel Edmonds. Love to Duane Stapp for helping me find my way and being the best walking companion ever, and to Tyl Stapp for all of the research and sourcing. Many thanks as well to Aubrey Thelonious, Bonnie Pitman, Crystal Sershen, Danelle Davis, Kimberly Brown, Magdalen Beiting, and Shamini Jain. And in remembrance of Ruth Mullen and the walks we took and the ones I wish we had.

Picture Credits